The Master's Word

A Short Treatise on the Word,
the Light, and the Self.

Addressed to Rosicrucians and
Freemasons wherever they
may be dispersed,

BY

GEORGE WINSLOW PLUMMER, *F.R.C.*

NEW YORK:
GOODYEAR BOOK CONCERN
1913

Copyright, 1913,
By George Winslow Plummer,
New York City, N. Y.

Imprimatur

M.: W.: K. Imperator.
R.: W.: A. Praemonstrator
R.: W.: H. Cancellarius.

CONTENTS

PREFACE

In offering this little treatise on the Three Cardinal Points to my Rosicrucian Fraters and Masonic Brethren, it is incumbent upon me to explain to some extent my reasons for so doing.

Both Orders are essentially esoteric. With a lineage, however, crowned with the dignity of remote antiquity, their Convocations and Communications have become largely ceremonial sessions.

It is with the hope that this book will meet a long felt want on the part of some, and stimulate others to independent thought and research that it is sent forth to do its work among the Brethren.

It is not possible that the Author will ever know the results attendant upon its reading, in the majority of cases. He would not desire to do so. To those who seek "further Light" it will be warmly welcomed. By the orthodox and the slaves of creed it will be strongly condemned as heretical and atheistic. As a matter of fact it is neither, for the Author has approached this work solely as a student, actuated by a sincere desire to learn and to give forth only the Truth.

PREFACE

It is only right at this point to express my sense of gratitude and obligation to the works of E. H. Britten, John Fiske, R. W. Emerson, Ernst Haeckel, Giordano Bruno, Paracelsus and Edward Westermarck, whose inspired lines have in many instances "opened the door" that more light might shine through.

The Master's Word goes forth as an Act of Karma. The Author is not solicitous as to its results nor does he seek pecuniary gain. To all to whom this book may come the Author sends with it the strongest vibrations of good-will and desire for the advancement of independent thought.

George Winslow Plummer.

New York City, January, 1913.

INTRODUCTION

FOR countless aeons that Word, which, we are told by the seer, had its primal association with the Great Architect of the Universe, has gone crashing through the boundless realms of infinitude, obediently fulfilling the Divine Mandate, "Let there be Light."

Countless suns, systems, and universes have sprung into being, each continuing the work which was the purpose of its birth. If geological science fails us not, upwards of 350,000,000 years ago our ·own tiny planet gradually assumed shape, in order that it might deliver to its teeming inhabitants of future ages that wondrous message, which is not limited by the exigencies of language or the printer's art, nor written on the pages of any book prepared by mortal hands, but is spread upon the pages of the great book of creation. This message is interpreted through all the varying phases of life, organic and inorganic, so simply that its meaning is as accurately discerned by the ignorant savage, as by the most highly developed civilized intellect.

"Let there be Light, and there WAS Light."

The Word has gone forth; the message has been

given. From innumerable universes, of which our own is one of the least, whirling and flashing with their attendant systems through illimitable oceans of ether, down to the most minute forms of organic life, the mandate has been reverently obeyed—with the homage due its deific scource—except by man.

And why not by him? Why has he, creation's greatest achievement, failed to grasp that great Idea, on which his own development, that of races and peoples yet unborn and, greater than these, the true knowledge of his own ego, depends?

After the Alpha we are told "there WAS Light." Why, then, has it not been discerned? Has it altogether failed? Or is it possible that it WAS seen by our ancient fathers and is revealed today to those only who shall be enabled to brush away the obscurity of vision and part the veil of materialism which, like a pall, has shrouded the human mind for the past eighteen hundred years? "Seek and ye shall find" is the command of the last Great Expression of the Divine Idea. In compliance with this command will be found the only answer to the questions before us.

Has that Light yet been sought? Have any yet found it? A short time after creation's dawn the Light became shrouded in darkness. The childress of men were left to grope their way as best they could, a few of them now and then, perchance, catching a glimpse which they have vainly tried to reflect upon those who should come after them, in proportion to the illumination they received.

We shall endeavor to sum up the factors of human achievement in all ages; to bring to bear the searchlight of science, the deductions of the philosophers, the teachings of the various creeds of organized religion, the prophecies in the scriptures of all races, the beliefs of the ancients, together with the inspired visions of poets and seers of modern times, to bear on these questions which are of such deep import to the human race, for its present and future welfare.

Consider that Light for a moment. In what sense is the term used? Conformably with the requirements of language we use it in an exoteric or esoteric manner as the nature of the context may indicate. A closer examination will show that in reality it has but one meaning and one use. It can be applied in but one way which holds with equal truth to any usage to which it can be put. Science tells us, that it is "that agent, force or action in nature by the operation of which upon the organs of sight objects are rendered visible or luminous." Again we are told, that it is life, existence, "mental or spiritual illumination, or that factor which makes clear to the mind."

Now, whether we regard its action in analysis

as being corpuscular or Newtonian, undulatory or
electro-magnetic, the result is the same, nor is its
meaning affected thereby.   If we owe the Order
which was evolved from Chaos to its action, the
orderly institution of the solar bodies of the universe in their respective spheres of activity, together with the concomitant creation on each, of
the conditions which have made it possible for the
life principle to reach the development we find
manifested in the highest types of mental equili-
brium of today, can we not see that no matter in
what way the results of its action may appear,
whether through physical or spiritual channels, there
can be but a single ultimate meaning to the term?

We shall try in the following pages to reach
that meaning. By divesting ourselves so far as
may be, of all preconceived opinions, secular or
religious; and from a cosmic, rather than a ter-
restrial standpoint, we may reach a conclusion.

It may be that the Master's Word has NOT been
lost forever.   It may be that inasmuch as all about
us we see its action and its results, the door may
be opened to him who knocks, and the seeker shall
find what all truth seekers have sought, too often
in vain, from the mystic priests of ancient Mizraim
and the sages of the East, down through the esoteric
brotherhoods of the Pre-Christian Era, Essenic and
Mithraic, the Apostolic Age, the Illuminati of the

mediaeval period, culminating in the wave of "New Thought" which is sweeping over Europe and America at the present day, and its attendant cults of mental and therapeutic suggestion, psychic phenomena, and the revival of occult brotherhoods.

To quote an old ecclesiastic: "I have sought the truth in the desert, in cities, in the universities, in communities, and cloisters: I have sought it at the feet of the Pope who claims to be infallible, and found it not. At last I did find it—I discovered it within myself."

So it is possible that every one may yet find within himself that Word which is truth. When we shall have found it we will not publish it broadcast throughout an unreceptive world, any more than our ancient fathers did in bygone ages. Rather will it be to us an incentive to higher attainments, broader pathways, and loftier aspirations. We shall then take up Creation's story which is not yet concluded, and be carried on, into a mental and spiritual outlook far transcending anything ever before experienced.

Light is not the exclusive possession of the initiate of any fraternal or esoteric brotherhood in this or any other age. He who would become truly illuminated must receive his initiation first at the hands of a higher authority than that of a set of annually elected officials who may or may not possess the requisite spiritual qualifications. True illumination does not require a belief in mythical mahatmas, nor does it require a spectacular ceremonial. A conscious revelation to the higher spiritual faculties and powers inherent in every human being it does demand, and this revelation follows upon contact with and knowledge of the unseen forces of the cosmos in and about us.

Creation's work is far from finished, even on our own humble planet. When we cannot fully know the past beyond hypotheses more or less tenable, how can we hope to see into the future unless through the aid of forces beyond the limitations of mortal or physical existence? Since the natal day of earth, continents have assumed shape and form which have vanished with their countless millions of inhabitants and civilizations of varying degrees, leaving behind them neither track, trace, nor remembrance that their existence might be known among men. Of these vanished lands, we have shadowy legends and mythological traditions which have furnished motifs to popular story writers. Of our present continents we have but the conjectural, the largely demonstrable theories of geological and archaeological science to picture to us their formation of even only a few thousand years ago.

To whom has the ocean revealed the secrets of

its hidden depths? To whom have snow capped peaks of Alps or Himalayas told a story of the awful cataclysms of nature which brought them into being? Who has heard of the fates of living creatures that swarmed the earth's surface when great fissures engulfed vast areas in their capacious maws? To whom even of our greatest astronomers has interstellar space told the story of its teeming life? Grave scientists tell us that above our atmosphere lies an empty void. Yet in the same breath they postulate as one of the unchanging laws of nature that she abhors a vacuum. Recently this paradox has been somewhat bolstered up by the various theories concerning the ocean of ether. If true, these hypotheses may yet reveal to earth's inhabitants in ages to come a vehicle of communication between them and neighboring planets in our solar system, which parenthetically may disclose our planet's tardy progress along the pathway of evolution, by comparison with our celestial neighbors.

Before our very eyes the pioneers in psychical research are opening up new worlds, by discoveries of conditions which are conforming to demonstrable laws. The results will rob the grave of its terrors and death of its bitterest sting. The message received by Prof. Hyslop from his dead friend, Dr. Hodgson, though no more wonderful than many received by less conspicuous persons in the acad-

emic world, will, with the first imprimatur of science
upon it, ring down the ages to come as the first
glimmerings of a new era.   What is it for which
humanity cries out today?   What is it for which
the world has waited these millions of years?   A
gospel, say some.   Yes, but gospels have come
and gone, and humanity still cries out, and the
agony of those aspiring souls, still held in mental
and spiritual bondage, is an eloquent testimonial
that not to creeds nor to founders of creeds shall
humanity owe its ultimate deliverance.

What is it for which the cry is being raised?
Light.   More Light.   Light on what?   On the
great mystery of life itself, which after all, is simply
the knowledge of the Self.   Who are we?   Whence
came we?   Whither go we?   We know not.   Yet
because we DO know the absolute indestructibility
of matter as one of the rudiments of physical science,
and that matter in its ultimate analysis is, for want
of a better term, pure spirit, so do we know that
by virtue of the undying, eternal nature of the life
principle, varying in the myriad manifestations of
its evolutionary career, that we are equally eternal,
without beginning and without ending.

Immortality is a FACT.   Unnumbered aeons
may have elapsed ere the life principle reached its
present stage of self-consciousness as a distinct entity, yet, once attained, this can no more be de-

stroyed than any of the other attributes separating us from the lower forms of life.

Nature's great law is that of progression. If millions of years have been required to bring to perfection the tiny grain of sand on the seashore, are we to assume that recreant nature would be so prodigal of her strength as to waste it in the prodigious efforts required in a correspondingly greater length of time, to bring the race of today, with its semi-divine attributes to its present stage of existence? When we consider the gulf between present man, the anthropoids, and the pithecanthropi; the gradual change in anatomical symmetry, the discarding of organic functions now obsolete, as the result of change in environment, is it unreasonable to infer that the human being of a few thousand years hence will have widened the gulf, producing a radically distinct type? Life is varying; it is progressive. But the point is, it is eternal. Meanwhile it may be that we of today, as well as those who have passed into the Unseen will continue our existence and progression on purely spiritual planes. Our progress thereby will be only the swifter. On the other hand, it may be that the species of ten thousand years to come, will have so far become illuminated that the line of demarcation between the physical and spiritual planes, will have become nearly obliterated. Thus the necessary duration of the purely physical existence will be correspondingly shortened.

That would be in obedience to the Law of Compensation. We do not know positively that this can be so. It is, however, a logical inference. As a matter of fact it need not concern us. If life, though it be varying, is unending, then immortality is a certain fact. Just as in every preceding change, it has not relinquished any of the attributes of its former state, but has taken on those of a higher, newer, and better condition, so it will not relinquish any of the attributes it has acquired during the purely human phase of existence. In discarding the impedimenta of mortality, it will invest those attributes with immortality.

This reasoning is not specious. It simply brings us face to face with one of our questions, who are we? It is all important for us to know. Can we but gain the faintest conception of our own spiritual identity, we shall in some measure have parted the veil which shields the beauty of the Unseen world beyond from the profanation of vulgar curiosity or mortal gaze. If we succeed in answering it, we may find, too, that after all there is no such thing as death. The word, as a result of the associations which in all ages have clustered about it, is a misnomer. We may be enabled to see that the instantaneous act of transition, during which the spirit or Self divests itself of mortality and puts on immortality, is but the passage whereby we at last gain a glimpse of our future habitation, where time is not, and whence we shall look back upon our earthly sojourn as with the sense of a long protracted visit from our eternal home.

THE VOICE OF SCIENCE

The human intellect is unable to comprehend in any true sense, the idea of a personal Deity as expressed in the formularies of the religious creeds of today. Many, both thinkers and the thoughtless, believe that they do, but as one philosopher has said, "Belief is the last resort of a fool." Absolute knowledge is the only measure of the soundness or fallacy of any proposition. Moreover, it is impossible for the finite mind to grasp in its entirety the Infinite. Therefore, our only conceptions regarding the Supreme Intelligence or Great First Cause must of necessity be purely conjectural, and any belief founded upon mere conjecture is hardly the rock on which to erect our spiritual temple, the "house not made with hands, eternal, in the heavens."

The belief in a Deific Being endowed with personality is largely an outgrowth of Christianity and Judaism, although the religious philosophies of the past have not been entirely free from it. The devout adherent of Christianity assures us with the greatest solicitude for the salvation and well-being of our souls, that we certainly know of such a Being through his son, Jesus the Christ. In reply we are tempted to ask, which son and which Christ, for this Being has many sons, and there have been many Christs.

While the writers of the Apostolic Era have assured us that God is a spirit and that those who worship him must "worship him in spirit and in truth," asserting his omniscience and omnipresence, they have also invested him with a personality which drags him down to the level of his own worshippers. A mythical Being, endowed with magical powers, to whose image humanity conforms, apparently constructs for no other reason than his own pleasure, our earth and other solar bodies. He peopled our planet and probably the others with living creatures, and then sat with infinite wisdom in judgment on the works of his hands and pronounced them good. But finding himself slightly mistaken, he proceeded to drown them from the face of the earth, except a saving remnant of one particular family with whom he was on intimate terms and from whom he rekindled the whole race. The second experiment is apparently no more successful than the first. Mankind is soon made aware, through prophetic messengers, that, through no fault of their own, the curse drawn upon the heads of their forefathers has been graciously saddled upon their own to cheer them on their toilsome march through mortal life. Their happiness is further increased by the assurance that, in ages to come, future generations will be "saved" by the vicarious sacrifice of an incarnate son who shall atone for the sins of humanity by being offered up to his own father, for that father's original mistake in creating such an imperfect race as mankind.

This hypothesis is no doubt shocking to the orthodox, but is it not the legend which will be discussed by future generations, with the same interest as, we now manifest in deciphering the legends of Osiris or of Shamashnapishtim? The problem here set before us is the search for the Omnific Word that went forth at Creation's dawn, and for its first result, Light. Then we are to apply that Light to the study of our own Self, if possible, to learn who we are, whence we came, and whither we are going. An old Arabic philosopher has left us the following paradoxical axiom: "Man learns his future by looking forward into the past." What can we see of our future by introspection into our past career?

In Man we find the Microcosm of the Universe, a universe within himself. Before he can arrive at a state of correct cognition of subliminal worlds and spheres of being that are intangible through the avenues of sense perception, he must be actuated by conditions existent in his own organism operating upon him from the invisible realms of Being.

In Man, we find the trinity of elements—Body (matter), Soul, and Spirit. This trinity is analogous to the grand trinity of being—Matter, Force and Spirit. Matter is that aggregation of masses, molecules, and atoms in the four states, solid, fluid, gaseous and etheric. Its attributes are indestructibility, extension, divisibility, impenetrability and inertia.

Force is the active factor generally known under the term, "Life principle." It is a mode of motion. It permeates and vitalizes matter, although it can exist for the purposes of exhibition without visible matter. Its attributes are attraction and repulsion. It is the eternally active principle which charges every atom and causes inorganic matter to become organic. It may be electricity in the air, magnetism in the earth, sound, heat, light. Its visible operations are seen in gravitation, cohesion, disintegration, and centripetal or centrifugal modes of motion.

"Spirit is the one, primordial, uncreated, eternal, infinite, Alpha and Omega of Being." It may have existed independent of Force and Matter, evolving both from its illimitable perfection, but

Force and Matter could never have originated Spirit. "Its sole attribute embraces and comprehends all others, must antedate and surpass all others, and is itself the cause of all effects. That attribute is Will."[1] And just as there are many ways in which the attributes of Force are perceived, so do many subordinate principles emanate from Will. These are Love, Wisdom, Use, Beauty, Intelligence, Skill, which can be resolved into the grand trinity of trinities:

> Wisdom, Strength and Beauty;
> Creation, Preservation and Progress;
> Life, Death and Regeneration.

That idea of the trinity has found a place in all the philosophies of mankind, past and present, and its expression has been vainly attempted by all the creeds which have obtained since man first gave his higher aspirations concrete form. In it is the real secret of Creation, the secret which Rosicrucian and Freemason alike have sought to inculcate in the elaborate symbology of their mystic rituals. In its correct interpretation will be found the Light we are seeking.

"The possession of a legitimate method of research is even more important than the possession of sound doctrine, since it is only through the

---

[1] E. H. Britten, "Art Magic."

former that the latter can be attained.   Clearly, we shall never reach Truth if we begin by mistaking our guide post and start on the road that leads to error. A false method leads to false doctrine, which, reacting on the mind, confirms it in the employment of the false method."[2]

So therefore we must for the nonce discard the theories of varying religious concepts and, by analysis of these conditions which today confront us in the present stage of human development, reach a basis of argument as to the origin and purpose of the trinitarian idea.   Such a basis is supplied by the postulate of the existence of a Great First Cause or supremely intelligent Architect of the Universe, under conditions which shall satisfy the requirements of the whole history of evolution.   This postulate should also afford us a working premise for what we may be able to predicate of the evolutionary developments in the future.

Man is a conditioned being, and he must recognize the boundaries of human knowledge.   Therefore, as he can know little outside of his physical relations the Absolute, after all the deductions ,of science, must be incomprehensible to him.   The scope of his legitimate inquiry is coextensive with the existence of the conditioned and relative opper-

[2] John Fiske.

tunities of physical and spiritual perception. He who can grasp this truth will appreciate Goethe's lines: "The most beautiful fortune of thinking man is to have fathomed the fathomable and to restfully worship the Unfathomable."

To return to our concept of the primordial trinity, we may postulate an unfathomable condition, incomprehensible to mortals, and of Pure Spirit. Its single attribute is unconditioned Will. This attribute contains within its own indefinable perfection the latent possibilities of evolutionary development. From its subordinate principles we may be justified in assuming that Will operates intelligently through Love and Wisdom for Use and Beauty. Thus through the first section of the triple trinity, Wisdom. Strength and Beauty. by virtue of its inherent energy Force, the evolution of Pure Spirit will proceed along the orderly lines of Creation. The visible and invisible modes of its evolutionary manifestations, support and preserve the structure it is erecting by the increased strength it attains in the constant unfoldment to higher forms and planes. It beautifies its works by obedience to one of its cardinal principles, that of Conformity to Type.

This can in no wise be more aptly illustrated than by recent scientific revelation in the discovery of radium. This substance, tangible, yet intangible, whose origin is still a matter of speculation, contains within itself inherent energy which manifests in the radio-active form of constant emanations of portions of its own substance with no apparent diminution of bulk. So without attempting a classification and enumeration of the infinitesimal steps along the pathway of evolution, we may briefly postulate that Force, acting in obedience to conscious, intelligent Will, operates through centrifugal and centripetal modes of motion and vortexian processes upon primordial spirit substance. Through condensation of spirit substance into visible forms. etheric, gaseous, liqueous and solid, Force has produced suns, universes, planets and their satellites. On each of these bodies it has continued the same process, where by following the line of least resistance, it has evolved first the various forms of inorganic life, thence through varying stages of transition, the organic. Force has thus produced mineral, vegetal, animal, and finally the human species, in accordance with the third member of the second section of the trinity—Progress or Evolution.

Practically, then, our conception of Deity or God must perforce be that of the Basic Reality manifesting through the unknown factors Matter, Force and Spirit. Unknown, because we cannot certainly know what either of them are; neither do we know how motion originates. We, however, do know their properties. We know that Matter is indestructible, that Force is indestructible, "persistent, conserved," and that motion is continuous. Neither is space empty; it is filled with ether which is the great storehouse of those manifestations of Force known as electric and magnetic vibrations. This brings us to the present scope of action, where the drama, if so it may be called, is made up as follows:

Scene of Action—The Earth whirling through space.

Time Covered—Countless millions of years.

Dramatis Personae—All the countless inhabitants of all the myriad species that ever existed on earth.

Motif—The "Struggle of Life."

Finale—A Psychozoic World: Man, its Microcosm.[3]

The operation of the Will of the Basic Reality or Supreme Mind is made known to us through the following law of organic evolution: "Organic evolution consists in the differentiation of organic energy from inorganic energy and matter, through a transformation of inorganic energy and matter into organic energy."[4]

We come now directly to the closer intimacy

[3]Organic Evolution, p. 68.
[4]Ibid, p. 61.

with the human being *per se.* "From god, the
Macrocosm, to Man, the Microcosm, though spanning the Royal Arch of unknown chiliads of years,
is an appreciable step.   Man, the conservator of
all forces, the image of all objective forms, and
the embodiment of all subjective ideas,"[5] becomes
"the connecting link between all existences higher
and lower than himself."[6]   For in him, analogous
to, and the direct result of, the operation of his
Deific Creator, we find a change in the trinity of
his existence.   Until now it has been Matter, Force
and Spirit.   In him it now becomes Matter, Spirit
and Soul.   In his physical aspect we observe the
operation of the Deific Trinity, in a sense the incarnation of that trinity; Spirit or the animating
principle, made up of all phases of the forces we
call life; Matter, indestructible, and comprehensive
in its attributes; and lastly a third principle that we
designate as Soul.

Soul, the link which unites the creature to the
Creator, is the immortal essence of the Divine Trinity which survives all change.   It is not subject to
disintegration, and is the guiding and directing
power of the primal trinity, through the works of
its creation, up to its highest product, Man, in whom
the final triumph is attained—the development of

---

[5] E. H. Britten.
[6] Ibid.

self-consciousness and the evolution of an individual entity.

In all conditions of life we find *conscious* obedience to natural law.   In the lower forms of invisible matter it operates through the physical laws by which force itself is governed; in the next, to the law of Conformity to Type or species; in higher forms to the Law of Procreation or the perpetuation of species; in still higher, to that of conscious motion and selection.   In an ascending scale we find successively the Laws of Chemical Affinity, Adaptation to Environment, and Communal Growth largely operate to point out the pathway for the evolution of the life principle, until, in the animal types, it assumes that condition which we designate as instinct.

The line of demarcation between instinct and the analogous condition in the purely human species is very finely drawn.   It is well known that the developed instinct of the most advanced type of ape is superior to the intelligence of the lowest forms of human life, for instance such as the Australian Bushman.   Soul is not mind nor is it intelligence. · Mind and its attribute, intelligence, may be called the physical manifestations of soul. Soul is the essence, the Divine spark.   Back of and dominating the primal trinity, even as it does the trinity of humanity, it is the individual ego in many

portions and under many aspects, as racial types
increase.   In the evolution of the lower forms of
instinct into the higher form of reason or the ability
to make conscious use of the various avenues of
sense perception, it becomes a distinct and separate
entity, self-conscious and indestructible, therefore
immortal.

This high function is reached by the human
species alone. The human may be likened to a
horse and wagon and its driver.   The body represents the wagon or other vehicle; the spirit or
life principle, the horse; while the soul typifies the
driver or directing intelligence.   While it will be
seen that it is possible and probable that many
of the higher forms of animal life, in a lesser and
varying degree, do appear to possess the rudiments
of reason, yet the evolution of soul into separate,
conscious, individual existence can take place only
in the human species, as is evidenced by the fact
that only the human species are able to divine
the existence of an individual soul.

Man cannot, indeed, by sensuous perception ap-
prehend the existence of his own soul.   But by
the exercise of that reason which is denied to lower
forms, he can focus the inner Light, which is one of
our objective points, upon the conditions of his existence, so that its presence cannot be escaped. And
this has always been true.   Socrates declared this

truth when he said: "I respect my soul though I cannot see it." The apostolic or rather, Gnostic, writer, Paul, appreciated the same truth, when he said that the spiritual man could alone discern the things of the spirit. It is through the knowledge of the soul that we are to gain a knowledge of the Self.

Is it not reasonable to infer, since the same law that shapes the dew-drop, shapes a world, that the same principles which inhere in one solar system prevail throughout all universes in correspondingly higher or lower forms, according to the age and magnitude of any given planet. In such research, science and spiritual revelation go hand in hand. Physical science tells us it must be so. Spiritual science affirms that it is so. If religion urges science to accept the beginning of the world as 4004 B. C., when many of the Egyptian monuments antedate that period by over fifteen hundred years, and Egyptian and Babylonian civilization by a much longer period, there will be a manifest disagreement.

But when both lay aside their weapons of warfare and insist upon the truth only, there will be found harmony prevailing. Science is not loath to acclaim the truth when once it has reached truth. Geology, indeed, shows us the sure foundation on which our terrestial lodge is built, laying before our vision its various strata from the surface almost

to the centre, each marking, as it were, the various
birthdays of our planet.   Astronomy, scanning
the starry canopy which forms the ceiling, marks
the courses of the spheres with mathematical precision, and shows us new worlds in the making.
Paleontology points proudly to the fossiliferous
footprints of the pithecanthropos or antediluvian
man and gives us indisputable evidence of the
Genesis of Species.   Geometry enables us to learn
the attributes of the Great Architect of the Universe, and reveals the plans on the celestial trestle
board.   Medical biology shows us that the brain
of the human foetus in its progressional development resembles successively the forms of evolutional
development of animal life, thus proving beyond
doubt that man IS the microcosm of creation, sum-
ming in himself all the myriad types through which
the life principle has passed.   Archeology enables
us to follow in the footsteps of our ancestors through
the civilizations of the past. Microscopy reveals to
us the embryonic worlds contained in the tiniest
cell.   All combined show us the various changes on
the stage of the drama of life, from the struggle
for life which caused the reclamation of continents
from the watery envelope of earth in its dawning
eras, to the time when other conditions necessary
as the result of diminution of solar heat, exhaus-

tion of the coal strata, and loss of forest vegetation, shall ensue.

In all these voices, science speaks in no uncertain tones. Aside from doctrine and dogma, she gladly co-operates with religion—with this difference: science, albeit many mistakes, progresses; religion retrogresses. Science works along Nature's Law of Evolution; religion combats every advance, for fear of some pseudo essential doctrine being made obsolete thereby. Science satisfies the intellect of modern man. Religion seeks to enthrall it. In a thousand or two thousand years the average intellectual faculties of man progress. Religion ignores this progress, and seeks to thrust on man of today the dogmatic assertions of mediaeval ages, in spite of their too apparent fallibility. This should not be so. The reason it is so, is that all religions have been built upon the personality of a human founder, and as such are bound to stand or fall according to the status of that personality.

No human personality is sufficiently strong to attain immortality under mortal conditions and in mortal environment. Faiths erected on such are but houses built upon sand; and when the floods of scientific knowledge sweep over them they cannot be expected to survive the shock. Religion is the aspiration of the individual soul for a recognition, first of its own existence, then of its Creator's.

Religion comes from within and all extraneous embellishments serve to reduce to a mechanical process those conditions of mental evolution which should bring man to a true conception of the Supreme Mind, and by so doing, to a correct knowledge of himself.

"Know thyself" was the command of the ancient sage, and the world would do well to listen and profit thereby. Science, too, is at fault in many respects. Instead of scattering its energy in many directions, seeking many goals without one definite end in view, it should conserve that energy, employing it in as many differing pathways as may be indicated, but always with the certain aim before it of ascertaining the relation of the human ego to its environment, celestial and mundane. While any attempt to solve the mystery of life in a conscientious manner is always laudable, it will not be effected by fertilizing the eggs of sea urchins by radio activity, thereby proclaiming that the origin of life has been discovered, through eggs fertilized and hatched by artificial means; when the truth is that the tiniest cell in those unfertilized eggs already contained the germ of the life principle, and simply fulfilled the purpose for which it came into being, under artificial conditions.

"Seek ye first the kingdom of God, and all these things shall be added unto you." Man will learn of himself first from within, not from without.

THE VOICE OF PHILOSOPHY

Let us now turn to the speculations of philosophic inquiry and see in what measure the Light has been perceived by those who labor in this field of thought.

"The Newtonian system of stars and suns, let that be to you the fabric of your immortality, of an everlasting progress, and an upward flight. The planets of our solar system are bound to each other and their focus the sun, by the power of attraction. Yet the planets are the mere staging of the theatre; the mere dwelling places of the creatures upon them; who in varying degrees of distance, with ellipses, revolve around the infinitely more beautiful Sun of Eternal Goodness and Truth. Is it possible that the scenes themselves should be so closely connected, and not the contents of the scenes? Is it to be supposed that the planets are so exactly arranged in relation to each other and the sun, and that the destiny of those who live on the planets, for whose sake the planets were prepared, is not as closely conected? In Nature everything is connected, like body and spirit. Our future destination is a new link in the chain of our being, which connects itself with the present link most minutely, and by the most subtle progression: as our earth is connected with the sun, and as the moon is connected with our earth. When death bursts the bonds of limitation, God will transplant us, like flowers, into quite other fields, and surround us with entirely different circumstances. Who has not experienced what new faculties are given to the soul by a new situation?—faculties which, in our old corner, in the stifling atmosphere of old circumstances and occupations, we had never imagined ourselves capable of? In these matters we can do nothing but conjecture. But whatever I may be, through whatever worlds I may be led, I know that I shall remain forever in the hands of the Father who brought me hither and who calls me further on."[7]

What greater inter-corroboration of philosophy and science can be desired? Herein the philosopher-seer has discerned the indestructible individuality of the Self. The Traveler obedient to Nature's laws is subject to the influences of environment, always in the straight line of progression. In spiritual and mortal vision combined he looks back

---

[7] Johann Gottfried von Herder.

through the shadowy pathways of the past, with perfect confidence, and forward, in anticipation to that glorious East, wherein rises the Sun of Eternal Goodness. Has the philosopher seen the Light? Can we doubt it? Yet wherein does his vision differ from that of his fellow men? Schopenhauer has said: "Every one feels that he is something other than a nothing animated by another." From this arises in him the confidence that death, though it may end his physical expression, cannot interrupt his sub-liminal consciousness. Therein lies the answer to these questions. It is the voice of the Self, the Master's Word, which went forth at Creation's dawn no longer confined to the ordering of new universes; but, spanning the gulf which separates the physical from the spiritual, it solves for the true initiate the mystery of his being. It teaches him that he is more than potter's clay, animate, perhaps, yet subject to change and the processes of disintegration. It rends the veil of materialism from his spiritual vision and reveals to him the glories of his wondrous career throughout eternal ages past, present and future. Past, present and future? We use these terms as stepping stones only, along the pathway of our life's progress, for to the hierophant all three have long since ceased to exist. It is true that there is, indeed, progression of incident as measured by mortal standards, but to him who has seen the Light in very truth, mortal existence is but one of many phases of an absolutely continuous existence, of which any given point is but the Present, the eternal NOW.

He is indeed a true Brother who realizes the truth hidden in this occult verbiage: "He will be present in the body in such wise that the best part of himself will be absent from it, and will join himself by an indissoluble sacrament to divine things, in such a way that he will not fear either love or hatred of things mortal. Considering himself as the master, and that he ought not to be servant and slave to his body, which he would regard as only the prison which holds his liberty in confinement, the glue which smears his wings, chains which bind fast his hands, stocks which fix his feet, veil which hides his view. Let him not be servant, captive, ensnared, chained, idle, stolid, and blind; for the body which he himself abandons cannot tyrannize over him; so that thus the spirit in a certain degree comes before him as the corporeal world, and matter is subject to divinity and to nature. Thus he will become strong against fortune, magnanimous to injuries, intrepid toward poverty, disease and persecution."[8]

Moreover, Southey testifies: "It is only our

---

[8]Giordano Bruno.

mortal duration that we measure by visible and measurable objects; and there is nothing mournful in the contemplation for one who knows that the Creator made him to be the image of his own Eternity, and who feels that in the desire for immortality he has sure proof of his capacity for it." So from sage to sage comes the universal testimony to the existence of the imperishable, immortal Self, the Divine Spark, which, in comprehending within its own attributes the entire Cosmos, is in very truth the image of its Great Author.

When we view man, "comprehending in his single conception the events of ages which have preceded him, and not content with the past, anticipating events that are to begin only in ages as remote in futurity as the origin of the universe is in the past, measuring the distance of the remotest planets, and naming in what year of other centuries the nations that are now gazing on some comet are to gaze on its return, it is scarcely possible for us to believe that a mind which seems equally capacious of what is infinite in space and time should be only a creature whose brief existence is measurable by a few points of space and a few moments of eternity."[9]

Can anyone within or approaching the pale of

---

[9]Dr. Thomas Brown.

spiritual illumination fail to perceive the Light which shines through these inspired lines, to realize the infinite yearning for knowledge of the imperial Word, and to feel the prompting for obedience to it? The echo of this Word he can barely comprehend, though he be impelled thereto by the consciousness of an inner Self acting upon his corporeal substance.

Consider how that great trinity, the Word, the Light, and the Self, illumines the following lines by Carlyle: "Generation after generation takes to itself the form of a body, and issuing forth from Cimmerian night, appears on heaven's mission. What force and fire in each he expends. One grinding in the mill of industry; one, hunter-like, climbing the Alpine heights of science; one, madly dashed to pieces on the rocks of strife, warring with his fellow; and the heaven-sent is recalled; his earthly vesture falls away, and soon, even to sense becomes a shadow. Thus, like a God-created, fire-breathing Spirit, we emerge from the Inane; we haste stormfully across the astonished earth; then we plunge again into the Inane. Earth's mountains are levelled, and her seas are filled up, in our passage. Can the earth which is but dead, and a vision, resist Spirits which have reality and are alive? On the hardest adamant some footprints of us are stamped in. The last rear of

the host will read traces of the earliest van. But
whence? O Heaven, whither? Sense knows not;
faith knows not; only that it is through mystery into
mystery, from God to God."

If inspiration was ever doubted, is there not
abundant refutation in these words? From the
smallest amoeba to man do we not find the same
testimony—that of a conscious ego struggling up
life's pathway for separate, individual existence,
groping blindly for the Light? From Chaldean and
Assyrian cuneiform inscription to Egyptian hiero-
glyphics, do we not find the same conscious struggle for existence expressed, which, as has been
postulated, forms the motif of the great drama of
life?

"Out of the East cometh wisdom." The nations
of the East have ever led western civilization in
ability to read aright creation's story. This is as
true today as in the remote past. The principle
of the conscious struggle for existence has prevailed
from the earliest periods in Egypt, where extraor-
dinary attempts were made to preserve the erst-
while "temple of the soul," to the present code in
India, Egypt's pupil and proselyte, where all forms
of life from the humblest to the highest are held
sacred. This principle means that the rights of a
conscious ego struggling for existence should be
respected.

Christianity has not been altogether a blessing, for, while it has laid down precepts of a high moral order, it has selfishly arrogated to its human followers the rights only of individuality and egoistic existence. The proudest and most self-contained Christian drives to his place of worship behind horses mutilated in the name of fashion against all laws of nature. He "improves" his canine friends in the same manner. He ruthlessly exterminates with iron hand all those he considers unnecessary. to his pleasure or welfare. Is this the result of his moral guidance? As a man thinks, so (does) he.

This presents another problem to us which has a direct bearing upon the questions at hand. What is thought? "Thoughts are things," say those who gleefully pride themselves on being what is commonly termed psychic. Quite true. The statement is as definite and explanatory as though it were in answer to the question, "What are stones?" How few of us today realize the actuality and tangibility of our so-called thoughts? Today with elaborate and costly apparatus we can project through the air electrical vibrations susceptible of intelligent translation, without the employment of visible conductors. Many of us are sublimely unaware, however, that the vast ocean of ether and its almost magical functions and properties—that great storehouse of mystery which is just beginning

to be dimly revealed to us—is the greatest con-
ductor of all; for who can tell but that the forces
we so vaguely term electricity and magnetism may
have their home therein?   Do we compare this
vaunted achievement of our modern civilization with
the ability of the ancients to communicate across
still greater areas without the use of any mechanical
apparatus whatever?   In their case, through cere-
bral activity alone, one mind spoke instantly to another mind.

This is not a miracle of the pre-Christian era,
for today, in many parts of the far East, the operation of this same power on the part of native as-
cetics has been attested by men eminent in science,
connected with the British occupation of those sec-
tions.   No human brain ever orginated a thought.
The brain is merely the mechanism which, when
properly attuned, receives the vibration and trans-
lates it to our physical senses according to our
abilities and requirements.   The same vibration
may fail to impress one organism and become of
no account, like the expended force of wave motion
broken against the solid rock on which it beats.   On
the other hand it may afford an inspiration to him
who can receive it intelligently.   Who of us has
not witnessed the phenomenon of many men in
many countries, each totally unacquainted with the
other, diligently at work on one and the same great

problem of science, inventive or theoretical, that they have set themselves to solve? Whence came this thought? True, it is a product of their own brains in one sense, but whence did their brains receive the original impression?

Is it not patent to all that a common thought must have a common origin? The question is often propounded to students of psychical research, "Why does not the spirit world give information of scientific value to humanity?" The query is apropos of that concerning thought. The Unseen World does give all the information humanity can desire, but not in a miraculous manner, not by special revelation. It gives it through the channels and organic functions with which humanity has been equipped, and only as humanity has earned the right to it and progresses sufficiently to be able to utilize it. Every invention and achievement is inspired directly from the other side of life. Until man has earned it by a proper development he could not appreciate it, and it would therefore be lost upon him.

Knowledge is attained only as man advances and is ready for it. The proverb of ancient wisdom: "There is no new thing under the sun, no not one," is perfectly true. In no single instance can we point proudly to its Alpha and Omega. From the war chariot of Roman Caesar to the giant loco-

motive of today thundering across the continent,
all have existed in Eternal Mind throughout eternal
ages. The screw of Archimedes was but the germ
of an idea received intelligently by the human organism, which finds its fruition in the ocean grey-
hound of today. But who shall say that Archimedes would have been enabled to construct a Lusi-
tania had the idea been given him at that time
or in his day? Thought does not reside perma-
nently in any one organism, for where we find one
man, or perhaps several, have grappled with the
same idea and failed, another, in future generations possibly, has received it and carried it suc-
cessfully into effect. The power of thought is
incomprehensible to us, yet can we not see what
a powerful agent for good or evil it may become?
Every impression received through organic cere-
bration will, if used conscientiously to the best of
our ability, whether we succeed in developing it
to its utmost or not, go traveling on through countless ages to come, bearing fruit which will redound
to the welfare of future generations; while vice
versa, the same impression corrupted through our
defiance of Nature's laws and our inharmony with
our environment, will become a weapon of destruction whose effects will be far reaching.

Thought, therefore, we may conceive as the
operation of the intelligence that is one of the prin-

ciples of that Will which was the single attribute of primordial spirit, evolving through all its creative works. If we look closer shall we not find that it is the same Master's Word, ordering the Cosmos and all its multitudinous forms of life, from ages past and through ages to come, which continues to direct man as its highest creative product in the use and guidance of them all. Is it not significant that here, too, is a manifest searching for the Light by some great organic principle, which, as we review past years, from the cave men of the Stone Age to the generalization of types and races today, seems to point to an ultimate merging of all races and peoples into one great type or product? This type is combining the attributes of these races, constituting its members little less than gods, each carrying out his divine mission to an extent altogether beyond our comprehension. A flight of the imagination, say you? Yes, but have we not with us today those things which doubtless were far beyond the wildest flights of imagination of our forefathers?

Could Petrus Stuyvesant, who a comparatively few years ago calmly smoked his pipe at the close of a day's work on his little farm in the humble colony of which he was governor and which had been purchased from its Indian possessors for a mere handful of clam shells, have dreamed of the huge masses of steel and iron that in recent years have been raised six hundred and more feet into the air over the very spot he occupied? On the other hand, would we blame Fulton now, as we undoubtedly should have done when his little boat "Clermont" steamed up the smooth waters of the Hudson, had he prophesied the huge ocean palaces that glide majestically up to their moorings, bringing commerce to this, the world's imperial city? Imagination does not call for derision, for mayhap it is but the foreshadowing in any age of still greater things to come.

Before leaving this part of our work, there is another factor, another voice, which properly belongs to philosophy, since it bears directly upon the three cardinal principles that are the motif of this work, the voice of blood. There is an old saying that "blood will tell." Let us listen to its story, for it is possible that it may have an important bearing on these principles—more than would appear at a casual glance. On turning to the scriptures or sacred writings of any age or of any race, we find that blood plays a most important part in its philosophy. Occupying a position of peculiar significance in the ancient initiatory ceremonies of the temple priesthoods, it has been perpetuated even in modern times, although its original meaning has been entirely lost. The earliest records known to man indicate its inception into special occult significance during the prevalence in antiquity of the various forms of Astronomical and Sex or Nature Worship, through the period when sacrificial rites required the slaughtering of animals of various species, and culminating in the rite of circumcision as ultimately applied to the human family.

From the discovery of the properties of blood and its functions, and the ancient theories concerning these, a curious analogy will be found to exist between the conditions surrounding it, and those attendant upon the evolution of the principle itself through all its manifested forms. Biologically considered, it does furnish a permanent record of evolutionary processes. It may be that as a "river of life" it will be found to fulfill the necessary conditions as such—nearer, in fact, than the idea so commonly used in the figurative language of various scriptural concepts would imply. Analysis of its substance under normal conditions as well as in the state of decomposition; comparison of the various manifestations of its nature, psychic as well as esoteric, will show that it has other constantly active properties than those merely of dynamic action and reaction through the various processes of absorption and assimilation, and in its differentiation as arterial or venous.

Beyond the consideration of its red and white

corpuscles, serum, haemaglobin and opsonins, if we compare it with that of the lower animal forms, and still further with the sap of various vegetal types, we shall find that both as a life principle and as documentary evidence of organic evolutionary processes, it meets all requirements. Pathologically its condition in the human body, while the latter is in a state of fever, paralysis, catalepsy, psychic trance, or under the influence of hypnotism or suggestive therapeutics, exhibits most interesting and instructive phenomena. A discussion of these pertains to a medical treatise and is only mentioned here in order to cite all the aspects under which blood may be considered.

Aside from observation of its normal condition, it often presents peculiar phases under abnormal aspects. This we see instanced in the case of vampires, and in rare cases, in some humans in whom an abnormal taste for fresh blood exists. One species of shark will refuse the food of their natural environment if the possibility of human food be in any way attainable. The so-called "blue blood" is more than a myth, for in those humans who by a long line of "close-bred" ancestors, embody many of the most desirable human attributes, we find a marked difference between their blood and that of the lower types of the human family. Thus it is safe to say that while the discussion regarding heredity is raging about us, it will be found in time, that the blood is the great perpetuator of the various racial and family characteristics.   It transmits them from one generation to another.   Psychically considered it is no less interesting.   It is a well established fact that the sight of freshly shed blood has produced deeds of heroism and bravery, in what were at the outset the most abject cowards, while on the other hand the mere sight of it will cause most women and many men to faint.   Then, too, the mere drawing of blood in so-called affairs of honor has by long centuries of usage been considered an atonement and the only means of satisfaction.   Wild beasts, if taken when cubs, may be domesticated, until the moment they gain their first taste of fresh blood, when they immediately become ferocious and are no longer safe outside a cage. It is more than possible that there exists a connection between the abnormal taste for blood on the part of some humans and the abnormal results of sensuality as instanced in all ages of the world's history.

From the esoteric standpoint we find blood has attracted the attention of philosophers and occultists the world over, in all ages.   The ancient law, older than religion itself, "Whose sheddeth man's blood, by man shall his blood be shed," has formed the basis of many of the moral precepts of dispensations, old and new. From the significant part it has played in the consummation of the nuptial rites of all races in all times, down to the mediaeval period when belief in its efficacy, in combination with the blood of animals, together with herb and mineral preparations, gathered under what were considered the proper planetary influences, it has been one of the principal factors in both civil and scientific codes of procedure. Among savages it formed the basis of initiation in what was known as "Blood Brotherhood," and in more advanced tribes found expression as a tribal or documentary seal.

Again, considered from the viewpoint of the cellular theory, it harmonizes with the various psychic theories concerning cosmogony and theogony, while its very color, that of the aura of primary humans, suggests a curious analogy between itself and that of the ruby, the jewel most highly prized by the ancient Egyptians and which occupied such a prominent place in their ceremonial forms. That it is subject to planetary influences is evidenced by its condition in many people under varying phases of the moon, while the conditions of weather and temperature and other climatic influences, each exert their external forces to produce results which are daily seen in those who are specially susceptible to changes in environment and habitat.

It is more than probable that the phenomena of

pre-natal influence and the possibilities of influencing sex thereby, may be directly attributable to this marvelous agent. In our own day one of the greatest achievements of science is the ability to solve the mysteries of many departments of criminology by the analysis of blood. Psychometrized by a genuine psychic, it has furnished invaluable evidence as to personality.

Now this enumeration of all the properties of this remarkable fluid would be incongruous at this juncture were it not for the fact that to the initiate of the higher degrees and to the student of the mystic ceremonials of all ages, it is patent that some subtle power seems to be inherent within it, which loses none of its virility as time advances, and to know which, must be studied from other than purely pathological standpoints. What is that power and to what law does it render obedience? Surely not to any known by man. And the only pathway toward the solution of our problem lies in the direction of a Rosicrucianism which, while mystic in the manner of inculcating its doctrine, seeks not to enthrall that doctrine from becoming of practical value to its follower. Yet, while all the world may read, it will be the illuminated frater alone, who will be able to penetrate its hidden meaning, for meaning there surely must be. Its ruddy glow which suggests the Light we are seeking, and the

very apparent conformity to law and obedience
to an unwritten mandate which all its properties
evidence, indicate the Word; and its power of trans-
mitting the characteristics of race type or species
points unavoidably to the Self.

The true Initiate will remember also, the fact
that the infusion of human blood into animal types
below the anthropoids, nearly always results fatally
to the type receiving it. Blood from lower
forms can be received into the human system and
assimilated, but not vice versa. This is because the
vibrations are far too high for the lower forms of
life. Therefore the blood reveals itself to us as
the true "River of Life" which acts as the agent
of operation of that Force in its differentiated modes
of motion, which preserves from one generation to
another the sum of the activities of Past and Present, continuing them to those types of life which
shall be the product of the Future.

The Rosicrucian who has learned the true inter-
relation of the Dense, Vital, and Desire bodies and
the manner in which they affect the Mind Body
and Ego will need no further guidance to show
him the particular potency of blood which is far
more wonderful than any of the properties known
to science or to religion. Then, too, the initiate
has only to recall the power of the blood to continue the thought forms and life incidents of a

given ego, from one incarnation to another, in the
cases of those egos whose re-entrances into the
human expression were in bodies resultant upon
the closest kind of family intermarriages.   Further
than this may not be indicated on the printed page,
but to the initiate, the pathway has been pointed
out and "whoso seeks shall find."

SEARCHING THE SCRIPTURES

For upwards of twenty dynasties the inhabitants
of the Nile valley and delta, drew their religious
inspiration from the contemplation of that same
trinity which in varying forms has persisted even
unto this day, the Osiric legend.   And the Light
contained therein, shines forth in the mangled
skeleton of the ancient tradition still perpetuated.
Osiris, the male principle, the father of the gods,
has a dual expression in the female principle, Isis,
by whom he gives to mankind the infant son, Horus.
By the machination of the god of. evil, Set, Horus
by Typhon is slain, and the mother, Isis, starts out
on her search through Amenti for her lost son.
Finding him, she seeks a means of restoring him
to life.   This is accomplished by obtaining from
Osiris his mystic name, the Master's Word, by virtue of which she raises Horus from the dead.   Having obtained the secret Word, she now becomes all
powerful with Osiris, and with him rules the Egyptian heaven, and ranks as the second of the two
chief deities in the Egyptian theogony.   Right
here it may not be amiss to state that the securing

of the Master's Word by Isis and her consequent exaltation to coequal divinity, is the real reason why the female aspect of Deity has always been symbolized as the Sophia or Wisdom.

To the Egyptians, as to all other peoples, their theogony served but as a basis for their outward conception of the cosmogony, for in the world's oldest book, the "Book of the Dead" we find it written, "I am the Self created, I am Yesterday, Today and Tomorrow; and I have the power to be born again.   I am the Hidden Soul,   *   *   *   I am the Lord of the men WHO ARE RAISED UP, WHO COMETH FORTH FROM OUT OF THE DARKNESS."

The religion of the Egyptians was both esoteric and exoteric; and the wisdom of the temple priesthood was far famed throughout the ancient world and is a source of wonder even to us of the present day.   It stands out clear and sharply silhouetted against the mighty panorama of the achievements of bygone ages, like an eternal beacon.   It flashed forth the Light of Truth by virtue of which its priestly guardians were able to rule their beloved land wisely and well, preserving it as an integral unit in spite of all adversity for many thousands of years.   Can we fail to perceive in the passage quoted above, from the "Book of the Dead," the Lion-like strength of the Mystic Word bringing to

Light the Self which is hidden from mortal vision? Is not the inherent power of a system which enabled the Egyptian Mesu (Moses), the priest of Heliopolis (erroneously claimed to be a native of the race he delivered from bondage), to work signs and wonders in the Land of Midian, still operative? Through all the vicissitudes of mortal time as shown by man's rise from his primitive conditions and aboriginal surroundings to the intellectual supremacy which today has made him the visible ruler over created things, this power is manifest. And from the cosmic standpoint, can we view as pagans those who bequeathed to us this wondrous Light, until we are quite sure we shall not occupy a relatively similar position to the inhabitants of ages in remote futurity?

Meanwhile we shall probably continue to rob and desecrate the graves and final resting places of those for whom, in our state of civilization, no law exists affording them the protection we give to the peoples of our own times. We shall probably continue to expose to the gaze of the vulgarly curious, the forms and faces of the mighty ones of the past to whom nations and empires did homage. And we shall find, too, that the dawn of civilization in that ancient land, heralded forth a truth which was undoubtedly appreciated then, far more than at the present time; that of the Divine Mission of the human species, the Mission of Mediumship. Through man the principles of the Eternal Ego become individualized spirit. Through him again individualized spirit returns conscious and developed, to its Deific origin. Thus from the original trinity of our first postulate, which, through all the trinities of the past has obtained even in our day, under the form of the Father, Son and Holy Ghost, we find a still greater trinity emphasized, the trinity of God, Man and Spirit. Let us observe the constant presence of this basic principle which underlies the teachings of all the Christs of ancient times.

Confucious brought the Light into China during the Chow dynasty, many centuries before the Christion era, and through his disciples Lao-Kiun, promulgated the following doctrine, which, translated from the metaphor of the time, will be found to reiterate all that we have been considering on the previous pages; "Tao" (God) "produced one; one produced two; two produced three; and three produced all things." Mencius, one of the most distinguished followers of Confucius tells us (371 B. C.) that he came during a crisis in the nation's history. "The world had fallen into decay and right principles had disappeared. Perverse discourses and oppressive deeds were waxen rife. Confucius was frightened at what he saw and undertook the

work of reformation." Today an empire of four
hundred million souls honors his name and rever-
ences his teachings and memory, and when that
mighty nation shall fully awaken from the languor
of its oriental sleep and test its powers on the external conditions of western civilization, as it already
shows signs of doing, those principles which have
preserved its integrity these thousands of years will
be found amply powerful to place it in the vanguard
of modern progress. The slumbering giant will not
always lie dormant, and were we not blinded to all
Light except the imperfect illumination which is
the product of an age of materialism, we should
find that many of the things which exercise our
vanity the most, had their origin in the land, which
perhaps not unworthily, has been called the celestial kingdom. And if the reverence of ancestors
which the philosophy of their system has produced,
is an offence to our supposedly enlightened understanding, what must be the effect on cultured ob-
servers in that land, of the absence of parental respect and of chivalry, both of which have been
supplanted by the western greed for gold? Confucius has not lived in vain, for in his simple yet
sublime conception of the philosophy of the Cosmos, he has left a priceless heritage to a nation
which well knows how to preserve it against the
encroachments of all external influences. Verily

the Chinaman has kept that which was committed unto him with a fidelity which shames our modern culture with its warring religious factions. And when scholarship shall unfold the sealed and Hidden Wisdom that has accumulated for ages past in the literature of that little understood people, we may beware lest our vaunted triumphs of philosophy, when weighed against it in the balance of genuine logic, are found wanting.

Zoroaster or Zarathustra, whom Hermippus of Smyrna places five thousand years before the Trojan War, became the founder of the national religion of the Perso-Iranian people from the time of the Achaemenidae to the close of the Sasanian period, and through the wisdom of the Magi which was an outgrowth of his school, has left us his message.

At the beginning of things, there existed two spirits, Ahuro Mazdao (Ormuzd) and Angro Mainyush (Ahriman), representing good and evil respectively. In Ormuzd originated Light and Truth, and possessing creative power, he manifested himself in Law, Order and Truth. Ahriman was the personification of evil. No religious system which has ever existed has succeeded in grasping so clearly the ideas of guilt and merit as the so-called pagan teachings of Zoroastrianism.

Man's life consisted of two parts, one of which

was the continuous existence on purely spiritual
planes, first in an unconscious and then in the
conscious state.   The second was the transitory
phase of mortality, during which man had the
opportunity to indicate the conditions which should
pertain to the second stage of his purely spiritual
existence, by regulating the actions of his mortal
or physical expression.   Fire worshippers?   Not
at all, in the sense ordinarily accepted.   Yet we
shall find in a later chapter that they had not only
preserved the Light that had been transmitted to
them from the Christs and Saviours of preceding
eras, but, more potently than all the former, they
applied the principles of the Divine Fire, the Great
Central Flame, to their ethical codes in a manner
which has survived even unto our own times, as is
evidenced by the attempt on the part of several
cults to revive the contemplation of its ancient
philosophy and the possibility of its application to
the present ethical environment.

The Light, the Word, the Self.   With what immortality do they stand clothed, as through all the
ages they speak in unerring tones the same message to mankind!   Such a message, with the sole
exception of the Hermetic Doctrine, is the only
revelation mankind has yet received or ever will
receive!   And how long shall that message be continued, we ask?   Eternally! shout blazing suns and

glowing universes, as whirling in their fiery pathways through boundless ether, they direct our mental and spiritual vision ever from mundane to super-
mundane conceptions. Eternally! shout the
myriad of meteoric sparks spangling the starry vault
on a cloudless eve, revealing to us the birth of
millions of embryonic germs of newer worlds in
futurity.

Gautama Siddartha, the Buddha, came and went.
And today hundreds of millions of human souls
hail his message as the advent of Light and Life
into the darkness of the mortal world. From him,
man learned that the three score and ten years of
human existence was not the summum bonum of
being, and that not one, but many existences
marked the pathway from life to Light. For while
none will dare assert that his complex philosophy
has ever been understood to its utmost value, yet
it was adapted to the psychological requirements
of the races who acclaimed him their Saviour, and
countless generations have accepted it as sufficient,
and withstanding all attempts at so-called conver-
sion, have deemed themselves the better for its
voicing. Under varying aspects the story is thus
seen always to present the same truth, no matter
what its apparel may be. Whether the Brahma,
Vishnu and Siva of the Hindu, or the great trinity
of Allah, Mohammed and the Holy Spirit, which

today is the religious inspiration of one hundred millions of devout Mahometans, its testimony is unfailing.   What organic principle underlies this great philosophic pageant?

The Gospel writer John says, "In the beginning was the Word." Knowing as he must have done the traditions and philosophies which, from long before his time, have been perpetuated until our day, he could have meant but one thing: the Word, which is the Alpha and Omega of all existence, and he firmly believed that the Great Leader to whom he owed allegiance was the last and only authoritative exponent of that Word. It may be that in the absence of reliable historical or other external evidence, we cannot accept that allegiance as he rendered it; nevertheless it is patent that some great upheaval in the ethical codes of far away Judaea must have taken place contemporaneously with his life and work. While Bible testimony is of little evidential value, we must in the absence of any other turn to it for the outline of the principal events which occurred about that time. In the first place we can hardly regard the man Jesus as the founder of the Christian cult, for several reasons. Its very name gives us the first clue.   From Theophilus, Tertullian, and Justyn Martyr, we learn that the original name was Chrestians (the good ones), which is from Chrestos, the Greek translation of the Egyptian Osiris Un-Nefer, i. e., "the good ones."   In corroboration of this interpretation, we learn from Josephus (Diss. I, Sec. I [1], p. 833), of "an eminent person living in Judea, whose name was Jesus Chrest, or Christ," and of a "numerous sect" called Chrestians or Christians.

So beginning with its Egyptian name, the Christion (Chrestian) church drew its essential elements from the following sources:

First—Philosophy and theology from Egypt.

Second—The Life of the Christ from India (Buddhism)

Third—Mysteries and sacraments from Greece.

Fourth—Church government from Greece and Asia.

And in proof of this, we find that the first Christian bishop (Demetrius), at Alexandria, testifies A. D. 180, that Egypt had schools of theology already established before western Christianity was even planted at Jerusalem.   The Christian church was not established in the latter city until A. D. 120, and then by missionaries from Antioch, Cesarea, and Greece; so it could not have been the cult of the original Twelve Apostles; and furthermore, as biblical testimony states that "His apostles disbelieved on him," so James, who became bishop of Jerusalem, must have been at the head of one branch of a cult which had a spontaneous growth in several places at once.

It is interesting at this point, to note the testimony of Origin, A. D. 230 (Comm. in Matth.. p. 234), concerning James the Just, brother of Jesus. It certainly sheds some light on the attitude of that member of Jesus' own family who was nearest to him. "Till the very holy house was demolished, he said, that these things befell them by the anger of God, on account of what they had dared to do to James, the brother of Jesus, who was called Christ; and wonderful it is, that while he did not receive Jesus for Christ, he did nevertheless bear witness," etc. Yet this same James was one of the principal Bishops, Apostles, or Disciples of his brother Jesus.

It is probable that James interpreted the Christ idea in the light of Messiahship according to the Jewish code. At any rate, it is not probable that he could have interpreted the Christ idea as Principle, the highest initiation of a given period. It is also improbable that he could have been admitted to companionship in his brother Jesus' studies among the Essenes, Mithraics and other arcane schools of the time. As Rosicrucians, we regard the Ego Jesus as the incarnation of the Christ principle, from the time of his baptism, to the close of his career as Christ and the resumption of his work as Jesus the later writer and philosopher. Of the years of Jesus' youth, regarding which the Bible is entirely silent, we shall say nothing in these pages beyond reminding the student of those interior sources of knowledge which have revealed to us his novitiate in the same temples along the Nile, where Pythagoras and the galaxy of sages derived their initial instruction and later inspiration.

The figure of the Jesus of the Gospels is drawn probably from several sources.   That there were many who were called Jesus and that it was by no means an uncommon name may be seen from the Apocrypha, while the personality with whom we have to deal is undoubtedly made up from the Archangel Jesua, the Jesua of Capernaum, which the Bible calls Jesus' own city (this could not have been if he was born in Bethlehem), and the life of Buddha and the Egyptian magician recorded in Josephus as crying, "Woe to Jerusalem."   Then again he is called the Nazarene, while the first supposed mention of Nazareth in biblical encyclopaedias is 400 A. D.   Then, too, regarding his death, the apostolic writers state that the Roman soldier thrust his spear into the side of Jesus while he was yet upon the cross, and thereupon flowed both water and blood.

And this notwithstanding that it is one of the

well known facts of science that blood does not
flow after life is extinct, so that the inference is
therefore natural that Jesus was not dead, and as
the oriental custom was to bury the dead within
three hours, there was plenty of time for his disciples to remove him from the cross and convey
him to the safety of the desert. We learn further
that after the crucifixion, James and his disciples
were worshipping daily in the Temple and were
not molested.   It is doubtful if we should have
gained much insight into the real facts, had not
the Jews as a race committed what amounts to
poiltical suicide during the last twenty years
through the schism bewteen orthodox and reformed,
thus affording access to their ancient writings and
emphasizing the factional differences which have
always appeared to exist among them from the
Pharisees, Sadducees, etc., to the present time. The
Jesus of the Gospel was probably a leader of one
of these sects, and Judas, the so-called betrayer,
was undoubtedly a leader of an opposing faction,
who, in defence of his own teachings, tried to gain
the influence of the High Priests to that end. That
this is so and that he must have been a person of
some consequence is shown by the Bible itself, as
it tells us that no one but the High Priest was allowed in the Holy of Holies, yet Judas went there
by night and met the chief priests. Another sig-

nificant fact is the silence of biblical criticism which
fails to mention the evidence that would seem to
show that John the Baptist was not born until ten
years after the death of Jesus.   Further, the Bible
is silent as to any details of the family life of Christ.
It merely mentions his brothers and sisters, and
states that Joseph "knew her not" (Mary, Egyp-
tion Meri, Ma, Mu, Mut, Moeris), until after Jesus
was born, presupposing that Joseph resumed his
conjugal relations with Mary immediately after the
birth.   Shortly thereafter Joseph drops out of
sight.   The passage in the Book of Revelations
where it speaks of "the land of Egypt, where also
our Lord was crucified," is also significant to
Rosicrucians.

Now far from attempting to deny the existence
of Jesus, it is our aim to know exactly what took
place in Judea at this time. , From the facts pre-
sented we may be justified in assuming from the
frequent allusions to Egypt, that the real Jesus of
the Gospels was an Egyptian priest of the highest
culture and initiation and the finest moral attributes
who, Josephus records, traveled from Egypt to
Judea and prophesied the destruction of Jerusalem,
saying that not one stone should be left upon the
other, and who attempted the reforms attributed
to him.   This is further borne out by the Roman
records which tell us of one Jesus, a reformer, who

was arrested for inciting the Jews to seditions against the Roman government. Then again, one of the requisite qualifications for apostleship was that the candidate must have seen Jesus face to face. This would have accounted for Paul's meeting Jesus in the Arabian Desert after the latter's supposed death, for Paul on his return states that he received his apostleship not from man, but from Christ (Jesus), yet he did not know the other apostles until fourteen years afterward when he went up to Jerusalem and met them for the first time. Even then, he tells us he withstood Peter face to face, showing that there was certainly not entire harmony between the original Twelve. Several acts attributed to Christ are also without explanation, either from internal or external evidence. Jesus takes two of his disciples and goes up on the mountain and is transfigured before them, talking with Moses and Elias. Then going down, he tells them not to say anything about it. Is this altogether explicable? In another instance he says, "He that dippeth in the dish with me, the same shall betray me." Yet the disciples immediately question, "Lord, is it I?" This under the circumstances would seem to us rather unnatural. A most interesting parallel to the transfiguration of Jesus which would seem to have been without purpose, is afforded by a similar act attributed to Buddha.

The latter, discredited at first by his parents, leaves home and years afterward returns and is transfigured before them, showing them his previous incarnations for the purpose of converting them to a belief in his divine mission; in which purpose he was successful.

The clue to the time and circumstances of the real death of Jesus is given us in the Pauline epistles, especially when we identify the Jesus of the Gospels with the Egyptian described by Josephus. The differentiation between the Historic Christ and the Jesus of the Gospels has been brought out strongly by Gerald Massey, and in addition to this, our viewpoint of Paul, not as an apostle of Christianity but of the Gnostics, gives a significance to his epistles not otherwise discerned.

In Corinthians, we find Paul collecting contributions for the sick brethren and "saints" at Jerusalem, and intimating an appointment in that city at a given time. He advises the married or unmarried to remain as they were for Jesus was coming again, apparently during their lifetimes. If Paul knew this at this time, he must have known that Jesus was not dead. Farther on we find a different story. He now advises the unmarried to take unto themselves wives, etc., for no intimation is repeated of Jesus' reappearance. Reference is made only to Jesus' merits and spiritual gifts. Fur-

thermore the epistles now take on a distinct note
of sorrow, conciliation, and explanation, rather than
the dictatorial style Paul affected prior to this part
of his writings.

Now the only inference from this is, that Jesus
was the leader of an attempted reform movement
for which Paul had been raising funds, which would
have enabled Jesus to return and carry on his work.
He must have arrived at Jerusalem too late, for
it is at this time that history records that the Egyptian was captured by the Roman soldiers and crucified, which also bears out the assertions of learned
Hebrews that the Jews did not crucify Jesus, but
that he met his death at the hands of the Romans.
As a matter of fact, it is now believed by many, on
excellent evidence, that Jesus died a perfectly natural death; that after the scene upon Golgotha he
was enabled to escape to the desert, and in other
lands resumed his work by writings which have
been preserved and which contain complete accounts of his work in Palestine.

Now while Paul had previously bid defiance to
the Jewish ceremonial we find him later paying
liberally for the Temple sacrifices and conforming
to the Jewish laws, and there is no record to show
to what other uses he might have put the money
he had collected. It is certain, however, from the
customs of the times, that Felix would not have

kept him a prisoner for three years had he been a poor plebeian without means.

The Jesus of Paul, not the Christian, but Gnostic apostle, and the Jesus of the Gospels must necessarily be two different personages.   Since the only citation in Josephus' works which assert the existence of the Gospel Jesus has been by most scholars considered a forgery and a deliberate interpolation, the occult hypothesis of Jesus the Ego, and the manifestation of the Christ principle grows stronger and more apparent.   The farther we travel in that direction, the closer we shall probably come to the true understanding of the work and personality of the Great Leader who manifested about the time we have been discussing.

This short digression from the main channel of thought is not without purpose.   It is not by any means an attempt to destroy or underrate the teachings of the cult which later generations have ascribed to Jesus.   But, strange as it may seem, more of mystery surrounds the personality of this, the last Great Saviour of Humanity than that which envelops any of the former.   Certain it is that a Jesus lived and taught in Judea at the time designated, laying down precepts of the highest moral order and in the most beautiful allegory, reiterating in exalted forms the Word, the Self, and the Light, and proclaiming himself the embodiment or incarnation of all three.

It is of interest and value to us to attempt to unravel in some measure, the skein of mysticism which has attached to him on account of the similarity of conditions that held with all the former teachers of the Great Idea. For all have been claimed a miraculous virgin birth, a flight into Egypt (i. e., the unknown land), trials in the wilderness, twelve apostles, transfiguration, trial, crucifixion, or violent death, resurrection and ascension. It is, therefore, legitimate for us to learn all that is available concerning the last of these saviours. Bearing in mind this parallelism, let us turn to the various religious formularies which have obtained from the earliest times, and see what Light they may throw upon our problems.

Before proceeding, however, it may not be amiss to point out to the novice or initiate the occult hypothesis held by advanced Rosicrucians, that the Ego Jesus, is simply the highest initiate of the Earth Period, who as an act of supreme self-sacrifice, has incarnated successively as each of the Great Messiahs of the world. By his exalted rank, therefore, he was able to extend the use of his physical body to the purpose of the Christ spirit or principle, who is the highest initiate of the Sun Period. The differentiation between the Ego Jesus and the Messiah Christ-Jesus was seen at the so-called miracle of turning water into wine. Prior to that time we are told that Jesus was obedient unto his parents. The Christ spirit entered into him at his baptism. Now Christ Jesus replies to the mother who could not understand him, Woman, what have I to do with thee? This Principle left him at Golgotha, entered our planet and became the Indwelling Spirit thereof. Whether Jesus survived the cross as many occultists now believe, does not affect his mission or the sublimity of his self-sacrifice. The point is, that the value of a true knowledge of the Ego Jesus lies in the fact that by his life he gave to us the completest record of the evolution of an ego to its highest development in this solar system. He gave us an example of the comparative perfection it is possible for every ego to attain; an example of the truest and highest custodianship of the Master's Word with which he had been invested and of which he had become conscious. He utilized its wondrous power, not for self, but for humanity; and because the exponent of the Divine Light which lightens the world, a spark of which is implanted in the breast of each ego on attaining individuality and self-consciousness. Therefore, far from being a waste of time or even a digression, it was necessary for us to come to a gradual realization of the sublimity of this last great teacher of humanity, by divesting him of the attributes with which he has

been invested by those who ignorantly worship
him.

It is not important for us to attempt to establish
accurate time data regarding the lives of the previous expressions of the Divine Idea.   We accept
the results of their works as we find them today
expressed in the philosophies which form the bases
of the cults still bearing their names.   In the Ego
Jesus, however, we find summed up the details of
their activities, and therefore to him, as the last
of the Great Initiates to incarnate, and himself the
last incarnation of one and the same Ego, under
varying names of Messiah of many races and lo-
calities, our attention has been closely drawn.   In
later paragraphs the Astronomical Legend, or Celestial Drama, on which the fundamental principles
of all subsequent religions have been based, will
be given.   While we are considering the personality
of the Ego Jesus, however, it is interesting to note
the Light which modern research has thrown upon
some of the traditions connected with his life.   Dr.
J. G. Frazer says, "* * * tales of Virgin
Mothers are relics of an age of childish ignorance
when men had not yet recognized the intercourse
of the sexes as the true cause of offspring.   That
ignorance, still shared by the lowest of existing
savages, the aboriginal tribes of central Australia,
was doubtless at one time universal among man-

kind.   Even in later times, when people are better acquainted with the laws of nature, they sometimes imagine that these laws may be subject to exceptions, and that miraculous beings may be born in miraculous ways, by women who have never known a man." During such periods of unenlightenment, intercourse was regarded as a matter solely for the gratification of the senses, and offspring was regarded as the sign of favor of the tribal god or fetich.   This was true in the case of both married and unmarried women.   For an unmarried female to become a mother was looked upon in many cases, as a sign of especial favor, and thus a peculiar sanctity attached to such offspring.   They were set apart as priests of the god or deity, and from this mythos developed the peculiar doctrine of Virgin Birth which has since been claimed for each one of the notable spiritual leaders who have become the founders of world-wide cults.

Again, the true date of his birth has long been a matter of dispute.   In this case the date commonly observed as the anniversary of his birth, namely, December 25th, is very largely the direct extension of the Astronomical Legend, although the exact date of its adoption into the calendar of festivals and fasts of the Christian church, must be gained from a study of the writings of the Fathers, and the records of the earlier Oecumenical Councils.

Clement of Alexandria sets it as occuring on November 3d, 3 B. C. The incongruity here apparent, is accounted for by the controversy regarding the Calendar. By other chronologists, the date is given as the 28th year of Augustus, the 25th of Pachen, the Egyptian month, i. e., 20th of May. This date is taken most probably from the records of the Basilidean Gnostics. Another date given is the 24th or 25th of Pharmuthis, i. e., 19th or 20th of April. The author of "De Pascha computis" Africa, 243, sets the true date as the 28th of March. Still other chronologists have formed quite a consensus of opinion on the date of January 6th.

Space and the purpose of this book will not permit us to go further into the details of the life of Jesus. We have, however, briefly considered his so-called Virgin Birth, Date of Birth, Mission, and so-called crucifixion. For the real truth, and esoteric teachings regarding his alleged physical resurrection the reader must probe more deeply into the records of the Hidden Wisdom. Our only purpose in entering so deeply into a consideration of the mythos attaching to the Ego Jesus is, not to detract from the value of his life and work, but to stimulate the student of occult lore, to a fuller appreciation of the importance of Jesus' Mission, from a better conception of his wonderful personality and his incarnation as one of the greatest Initiates this planet has produced, or rather evolved. Let us be disillusioned as to the claims that he was the ONLY Son of God, and see rather, that as the Highest Initiate of our planet, he has shown us our true positions as Sons of God, essentially equal, but not equally evoluted.

The first worship formulated by mankind was undoubtedly Astronomical. How, or on what lost continent it was first given tangible expression, we know not. It has been placed by occultists successively on the continents of Pan, Lemuria, and finally of Atlantis. We can only read its evidences from the hieroglyphical and alphabetical scriptures which have come down to us from remotest ages. Yet to primaeval man it is not unnatural that the phenomena of the starry vault above should have become to him an object of veneration, appealing to him during the formative state of his intellect as the revelation of the secret of his Divine Origin and the goal of his Ultimate Destiny.

From earliest times tradition has been more powerful in its effect than written codes, and our forefathers, recognizing this fact, took utmost pains to cultivate and preserve this faculty in its integrity. Hence from the priceless heritage of oral tradition which has been preserved to us by the peoples of the east even to this day, we may glean something of the nature and philosophy of this, man's first external manifestation of religious conceptions. To the primal nomadic tribes scattered throughout large areas, a common necessity became apparent for purposes of successful agriculture and herding, on which their very existence depended; that of not merely noting the separation between day and night, but also the constantly recurring appearance and disappearance of the planetary bodies and their influence upon winds and tides and other climatic conditions. Thus the major factor of our system, the sun, by virtue of its solar supremacy became through his life-giving properties the embodiment of creative power, and typified to them in his totality, the Deific source of all being. With this simple starting point, the whole stupendous system of astronomical worship, with the fiery scriptures of the skies for its bible, was evolved. The heavens were studied out and divided into geometrical proportions with mathematical precision. The power and majesty of the Sun-God, the softer radiance of his consort, the moon, the splendor of the fixed stars, the terrifying appearance of fiery comets, and the mysterious nebulae with their varying influences upon earth, its mighty oceans and its vast continents of semi-human, semi-divine inhabitants, were all seen to be units of a vast whole, moving through space in regions unknown and almost unknowable, yet all in obedience to the principles of the trinity of Wisdom, Strength and Beauty.

The ancients well recognized the apparent path of the sun called the Ecliptic, which at two periods of time crosses the earth's equator, and by the relative positions of the two bodies divides the year into summer and winter, with the sun in the aspects of south and north toward the earth. The ancients further defined the sun's path along the Ecliptic, as between two parallel lines sixteen degrees apart, called the Zodiac, which was divided into three hundred and sixty degrees, four right angles of ninety degrees each, and twelve signs of thirty degrees each. These signs were called constellations and derived their names from the climatic conditions upon the earth at the time the sun passed through them. In the January of our year the sun passes through the sign Aquarius, the Washer, or Greek Baptizo, so called from the heavy storms and rains which then prevail. It proceeds thence in February through Pisces, the Fishes, deriving that appellation from the dearth and famine of vegetation prevailing as a result of the accumulation of waters. In March, Aries the Lamb signifies the newly appeared products of the Spring. In April, typical of the reproductive energy of the approaching agricultural season, the sign receives the name of Taurus, or the Bull. May personifies the reconciliation between summer and winter, bringing forth the earliest flowers, and in token of the fraternal harmony existing, gives to its sign the name of Gemini, or the Twins. June, from the apparently retrograde movement of the sun dubs its sign the Crab, or Cancer. The burning heat of July suggests for its sign the title of the Lion, while the Virgin of August, the Scales of September, the Scorpion of October, the Great Dragon; the Archer of November and the Goat of December, derive their appellations more from fancied resemblances in the shapes of their constellations, than from coincident conditions upon the earth.

The four seasons each received an emblem, the Ox, Lion, Eagle and Man. The Ox prefigured the agricultural pursuits of spring; the Lion, the fierce summer's heat; the Eagle of autumn represented the flight of summer; Man, the water bearer, showed the floods of winter. The two seasons of summer and winter represented the two conditions of good and evil respectively. Therefore, when in the astronomical year the sun descended from the North at summer's close, to cross the plane of the autumnal equinox, it heralded death to the works of the great life and light-giver and the desolation of winter. When he ascended from the south in the spring to cross the vernal equinox, it heralded his triumph and glory in the rejuvenating power of spring and the promised fruition of summer.

On this theological foundation has been reared the superstructure of every creed and religious system that has prevailed on earth since the advent of the light of reason. The groundwork once prepared, the later developments of this idea became far reaching in their effects. Every star was believed to be a symbol of good or evil genius, and every constellation was a realm peopled by beneficent or malignant angels or spirits, as the case might be. The influence of these stars was exerted upon the earth according to the sign through which the sun was passing. Let us now see how the plot of this celestial drama assumes form and shape!

The leading figure is, of course, that of the Sun-God. Entering the sign of Aries, the Lamb, in March and crossing the vernal equinox he became the Redeemer of the World, its Saviour from the sufferings and privations of winter. His advent was hailed with rejoicing, for was not his divine mission wherein he should give to the hungry, restore the sick, and bring Light out of Darkness, already begun? The height of his career was attained in summer, at the season known in the language of the astronomical religion as the Betrothal of the Virgin of August, to the Lion of July. Then the Sun manifested forth his greatest glory and the miracle of the solar year had been accom-

plished. During the constellation of the Scales or
Balances the Celestial Hero maintained an even
pathway, until he reached the Three Ruffians, the
fatal period of the Great Dragon, Scorpio of October, and the two evil months, November and December. The Saviour of Mankind must now be
slain, crucified on the cross of the autumnal equinox
and descend into the south, the Hades, Hell, Ge-
henna, Sheol, or Pit, of many nations.

The dire calamity is announced by the appearance of a Bright Star known in the spring as Vesper,
or the Evening Star, and in the autumn as Lucifer,
"Son of the Morning." In the vernal season this
luminary heralds the approach of summer, and high
in the heavens occupies what we may call the Seat
of Pride. In the season of autumn it has changed
its station and appears low on the horizon, and
with its change of name it represents the Mighty
Angel who, through Pride and Ambition has fallen
to the lowest depths and has become the harbinger
of Greatest Evil. Appearing in advance of the
Dragon, it is assumed to be the Angel that incited
a third of the Heavenly Host to Rebellion and Dis-
obedience, as the constellation of the Great Dragon
is one of the largest and most powerful in the
heavens, and from the number of Bright Stars in
its train, it has been called the Fiery Serpent of
the skies.

Thus from the appearance of a group of stars has arisen the suppostitious existence of Incarnate Evil, the Typhon of Egypt, Satan of the Persians, Pluto of the Greeks, Old Serpent of the Jews and the Devil of the Christians.   Thus in October the Sun-God is put to death by the Great Dragon in the "Crossifixion" of the autumnal equinox, and cast into the hell, or power of the two evil months, November and December who, like two thieves, are crucified with him on the autumnal equinox.   In mid-winter under Capricorn the Goat, in ancient mythology the renewer of life, the Sun-God reappears as a newborn babe.   To the ancients the mid-winter cluster of stars represented a Stable, in which appeared the Virgin of summer with her companion Bootes, or the constellation of Joseppe or Joseph.

The legends declare that for three days the Sun appears to stand still, yet greatly "obscured"; that during this time He has descended to the Underworld (Amenti) and is lost to sight.   This, in the Greek mythology is accounted for by the descent of Orpheus into Pluto's kingdom, where, by his sweet music, he rescued lost souls from the portals of Hades.   The astronomical traditions parallel this by the assertion that the Sun-God went on a mission of Enlightenment to those who were held captive in realms of Perdition.   (He preached to the spirits who were in prison.)   On December

25th he reappears and is declared to have been born in the Starry Manger by the Virgin of the World, the Virgin Mother of the Zodiac. In all ages Egypt has been called the "Black Land" and the symbol of the unknown. And so after the 25th of December, when the Young Child is born, it was supposed that the antagonistic influences of January and February threaten his life. The Redeemer is in danger of the mighty power of the wintry King, so he is carried Secretly to the "Land of Egypt" until the danger is passed, when he recrosses the Equator at the equinox (vernal), rising from the depths of Egypt, and becomes the "Lamb of the World" at springtime, when He taketh away the "Sins of the World."

The Virgin Mother of the Sun-God next demands our attention. The figure of this constellation is assumed to hold in her hand a sprig or flower with which she invites a minor constellation Bootes or Joseph, and which from its proximity is regarded as her Betrothed. This figure also gave rise to the Legend of Adam and Eve, from the apparent seduction of the extended fruit she holds out to him. As a result of combining, therefore, all these units and figures of the Astronomical system, we have the annually recurring drama of the Birth of the Sun-God, of the Immaculate Virgin, the Flight into Egypt, the Twelve Zodiacal Apostles, the Sufferings, Crucifixion, and Resurrection, which forms the basis of all the religions of future times, and accounts for the common origin of the similar traditions surrounding all previous Saviours. From the women who wept for Tammuz, the Syrian Sun-God of bible record, the mourners who followed Isis in her search for the lost Horus, the attendants of Ceres in her search for Proserpinea, the devotees of Krishna, the Sun-God of the Hindus, to the Marys weeping at the Sepulchre of the Jewish Jesus, all have but followed the legend of the Sun-God as handed down and perpetuated amongst all nations and peoples.

To which shall we attach the most censure, to the peoples of the past who perhaps were ignorant of the real origin of their systems of religious expression, or to the Christian theologians who have appropriated the theology of the ancients and then call upon the Supreme Being to attest the genuineness of the personalities they have rechristened with new names and located in new places? To him who would fully appreciate the truth that we shall try to enunciate in later pages of this work, it will be well to thoroughly fix this legend of the Sun-God in mind; for, aside from all religious significance, it may be found to have an esoteric interpretation, closely bearing on the problems we have set ourselves to solve. Bearing in mind the last

trinity which the advent of man has produced—
God, Man and Spirit—we find it is but natural
for the human intellect to turn from the contemplation of the starry bodies and the Unknown Deific
Source they typify, to the study of those conditions which pertain more closely to his own imme-
diate environment, and himself as the greatest product of that environment. This movement found
its natural expression in the development of Sex
Worship.

That no nation of antiquity was free from this
stage of intellectual evolution is evidenced by the
presence of the emblems of the phallus, lingham
and yoni, on the monuments of all races. The
Cross, which is the object of veneration to the Christion of today, had its origin, not as the symbol of
the death of a malefactor, but as the expression
of the union of the male and female generative
principles thousands of years before the advent of
Christianity. The steeples of our modern churches
are but abbreviated phallic symbols. We find that
the veneration of the organs of sex as symbols of
creative power was, for ages, one of the basic principles in the evolution of man's religious conceptions. The Bible teems with it and the Rite of
Circumcision stands out with a prominence hardly
justifiable in all its pages. The scriptures of all
ages abound in references to the inculcation of its

principles.   Many of the most gorgeous pageants of history have been in observance of its festivals among all nations.   It is not our purpose to attempt a lengthy exposition of its modes of expression.   We mention it, in passing, only to show the close analogy between the units of the last trinity we have postulated, and the evolutionary development of the higher mental and spiritual faculties of mankind.

To show the persistence with which ideas of Sex Worship have obtained, when once established, in all ages, even to our own, witness the symbols of the Ox, Lion, Eagle and Man, which are seen to-day in the stained glass windows of churches, representing respectively the Four Evangelists.

Following the third section of our trinity, Spirit, we find man's intellect seeks a still further means of expression along more purely spiritual lines of reason.   Therefore, from the contemplation of the heavens, and next from himself, man turned to the great scriptures of Nature and her various works. He observed the operation of the same Creative Power that brought the starry universes and his own species into being, through all the visible forms of life, mineral, vegetable, animal; and he promptly and correctly ascribed to each type, therefore, the possession of a modicum of that same energy which, under the appellation of spirit, we regard as the life principle.

Just as some of the religious systems of today teach the existence of guardian spirits, and symbolize them by various images intended to direct the mind of the worshipper from them to the object they represent, so in the case of bygone peoples, this regard for the spiritual energy was expressed in the deification of various vegetal and animal types, symbolized by images of the same, and intended for the same uses to which they are put today. Nevertheless, the finding of such objects, in the desecrated tombs of their ancient possesors, has earned for them at the hands of this supposedly enlightened era, the titles of pagan and heathen.

Thus from Astronomical, Sex and Nature Worship, we see again accentuated the steps from Deity, the Macrocosm, to Man the Microcosm, which still later evolved into a higher form in the application of their essential ideas to the traditional personages of individual tribes, communities, and races, that gave to earlier times the cult of Hero Worship, from which the mythology of the ancients developed into the basic principles of the Age of Chivalry.

To sum up then, the work of the Great Teachers of Humanity in all ages, we find:

Osiris, demonstrating resurrection, immortality and judgment in the Halls of the Two Truths.

Confucius, teaching the continuity of life and the

obligation of continued respect for those who have passed beyond.

Zoroaster, or Zarathustra, and his philosophy of fire as the visible expression of Creative Energy.

Jesus the Christ, and his affirmation of the principles of all preceding philosophies, coupled with his further manifestation of the Deific Source as a spiritual entity.

Mohammed, with his denial of the divinity of any of the preceding teachers, and his affirmation of the existence of a monogamic Deity, with all the others, including himself as the greatest, the prophets of the One God.

Krishna and Buddha, teaching the truths of reincarnation and the peculiar sanctity of all forms of life, organic and inorganic.

All these philosophies have swept successively as breaths from the Unseen across our planet, each leaving its impress upon our civilizations and our intellectual development, until today a supernatural or supernormal religion no longer holds sway or binds the greatest intellects in its thralldom. So far as the tangibility or evidential value of physical environment is concerned, mankind has learned from it that after all, the only true revelation of the Divine Idea is to be found, not in any book, but on the pages of the Cosmic Universe, which lie open so that he who runs may read. The deep rooted and ingrained consciousness, common to the lowest savage and the highest type of intellectual development alike, impels each to a belief in a condition of conscious existence subsequent to their present mortal state in the investigation of which, the greatest psychologists our world has yet seen are but the pioneers along an untrodden pathway.

Religions have waxed and waned, but that only is eternal which has never been completely defined —Truth. The world is ready for a newer and higher civilization which shall be more than a veneer, conserving to its utmost the power of the trinity of Word, Self and Light, through a recognition and understanding of the principles of their Divine Origin and Nature; such a civilization as shall teach each of its units its duty and obligation to the whole body of its kind, because a portion of the whole; such a civilization as shall join in harmonious unity the whole fabric of humanity into one overwhelming fraternity, against which there can be no opposing forces. Why send we missionaries to those peoples who already have the Light, while we ourselves are yet groping in the blindness of darkness and ignorance, and mayhap, stand in much greater need of illumination than those who have preserved the philosophies which have come down to them through all the ages, unmutilated and ever increasing in their virility? What means it to our boasted civilization and culture when we find the despised pagans (sic) of far away lands, planting their missions in our very midst in a manner which leaves no doubt of their permanency? Why the turning to them on the part of many of our most cultured ones? Why the empty seats in the modern houses of God? It is because we are tired of the husks of an empty philosophy which does not satisfy, and because the external expressions of the Inner Nature are become but the stepping stones to social prominence and eclat. To the Initiate who has seen the Truth in the legend of the spheres we have related, and has followed it through the teachings of the Masters of old, has come the answer to all these questionings and has prepared him for the truest conception of the principles yet to be related.

LIFE, DEATH AND REGENERATION

Life is the Great Mystery of the Cosmos, which, from time immemorial has rivetted the attention of the world's deepest thinkers in the attempt to unravel the secret of its origin. From the royal astronomical priesthoods of antiquity, watching from their high towers and pyramids the movements of the Celestial Bodies, in the hope of gaining some clue therefrom as to their mysterious action; through all the forms of religious expression in the Bibles of Humanity, whether rituals of Egypt, Yih-King of Confucius, Persian Zend-Avesta, or veiled in the allegory and imagery of Vedas, Upanishads, or Dhammapada of India; the cabalistic formulae of Mosaic and Talmudic writings, Apostolic Epistles, Christian Parables, and Mahometan Koran, down to the researches of modern science, it has remained the question propounded by the Sphinx of the Universe unanswerable by the Oedipus of Humanity. And since it remains inexplicable by the laws and theories of physical science, whether atomic or molecular, or the results of biological analysis, the Neophyte in the Great College

of the Universe must turn to principles purely esoteric in their application in order to attain more
Light on its Nature and Attributes.

Mankind can never absolutely know WHAT life
is, for such knowledge would involve a comprehension of conditions so purely infinite as to be beyond
the attainment of finite understanding. We can
at best define it on a physical basis, as the dynamic
energy operating through all forms of Matter, visible
and invisible, including, for the time, in this use
of the term Matter, the idea of Spirit as living the
invisible substance. Philosophically we may define it from a still higher plane as being the visible
manifestation of Spirit or Cosmic Force, continuous,
and conserved in its energy.

One of the strongest and most convincing proofs
of its continuity and therefore immortality, is given
in our very inability to comprehend its origin, if
such it may be said to have had, although we are
totally unable to conceive of any condition which
might serve as a basis for its initial activity. The
testimony of the laws of organic evolution further
prevent us from conceiving even theoretically of
any ultimate condition which shall indicate a totality
of its development and attainment, thus again at-
testing its attribute of continuity or immortality.
Therefore, the only tangible idea we are able to
formulate as to its true nature is that of an eternally

active principle operative through all the departments of the Cosmos, making itself visibly manifest in Nature's works, which brings us back again to our starting point, the primal trinity, Matter, Force and Spriit, or in their totality the condition we term Deity.

The incarnation of this very idea, if we may be allowed to express it as such, is seen in the testimony of the Aitareya-Aranyaka: "The immortal dwells with the mortal, for through him (the breath) all this dwells together, the bodies being clearly mortal; but this Being (the breath), is immortal. These two (body and breath), go forever in different directions; the breath moving the senses of the body, the body supporting the senses of the breath; the former going upwards to another world, the body dying and remaining upon the earth. They increase the one (the body), but they do not increase the other; i. e., they increase these bodies (by food), but this Being (breath) is immortal. He who knows this becomes immortal in that world, and is seen as immortal by all beings; yes, by all beings."

It is not our intention to offer quotations from the Oriental Scriptures as scientific proof of such an abstract proposition, with the idea that it will be acceptable to the human intellect of today, but simply to show that the basic truths underlying them all have been dimly perceived and their expression attempted in all ages. Indeed, it would be a great mistake if we were to accept, for instance, the passage from the Bhagaved Gita which reads: "The soul is the principle of life, which the Sovereign Wisdom employed to animate bodies. Matter is inert and perishable. The soul thinks, acts and is immortal.....There is another invisible, eternal, existence, superior to this visible one, which does not perish when all things perish." And although Krishna exclaims, "All that doth live, liveth always," we can easily discern the confusion which must necessarily result from a too literal interpretation of his words. Soul is not life itself. Neither is Matter inert and perishable. One of the principal attributes of Matter is its indestructibility. Matter, resolved into molecules, atoms, ions and electrons, can at that stage be comprehended only on a basis of spiritual substance, and since we have postulated that life is the visible manifestation of Spirit or Cosmic Force, we find that Matter, instead of being inert is very much alive and imperishable. One of the greatest truths in the metaphysics of Christian Science today, is the assumption that all is Spirit. One of its greatest errors is the postulate that matter is non-existent. This paradox may be explained by the reconciliation of the two postulates in a third, namely, that mat-

ter is the objective manifestation of spirit substance.

Our research in this direction brings us, at this
point, naturally face to face with the reminder that
"in the midst of life we are in death," and it might
also be added, vice versa. If life is to be considered as the visible manifestation of Cosmic Energy
or Force, then the cessation of its visible manifestation must be logically, what we term death. Matter we know to be indestructible, and susceptible
to action and reaction and capable of entering into
new chemical combinations and affinities; therefore, it can never become non-existent, but can
only enter a new environment and take on new conditions. But we have also found Matter to be the
objective manifestation of spirit substance; therefore, its various properties must inhere spiritually
as well as physically. If life is the visible manifestation of spirit force, then the cessation of its
visible manifestations, which must necessarily be
indestructible, simply implies the transference of
its activities to another environment and under
other conditions.

As we have found that in the human, Spirit has
become individualized, developing its attributes in
a constantly ascending scale from one condition
always to a higher, what does our reasoning lead
us to? Simply the logical demonstration of the

immortality of the spiritual part of the human being, whereby so-called death becomes the release
from one set of limiting conditions and the en-
trance into vastly higher and more expanded conditions of existence.   Now, since Matter is Spirit,
and in its last analysis indestructible, and we know
by visualization that at least that portion of it which
is objective, is acted and reacted upon in Nature's
great retort, the earth, entering upon new combinations and environments; it is patent that a separating process has been experienced, by virtue of
which the more sublimated essence or spiritual
body has also entered a new environment or sphere
of activity, of a correspondingly more refined and
subtle nature.   In other words, while we have at
last found Spirit and Matter to be one and the same
under varying aspects, we find death to be the final
solvent whereby the grosser elements of spiritual
essence are separated from the finer, both continuing on the scale of progression or evolution but
in differing ratios, until in due process those elements having failed to develop in one set of experiences and in one environment, will in time have
reached the stage attained by those finer elements
which preceded them.

Thus, through life we reach death; through death
we attain regeneration or a still higher life, for as
in the individual body countless cells are dying

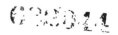

every second that they may give place to higher
and better types necessary to growth and strength,
so in the aggregate, countless humans (and in fact,
all manifestations of life) are constantly giving
place to higher and better types in the evolutionary
process.

Those of us who have passed from the visible
stage of activity have but passed to a wider sphere
of action on a much higher plane.   Regeneration
takes on a more important aspect when we consider what it means to the individualized Spirit,
after its long and tiresome journey through the
various kingdoms of life.

From primordial Spirit to the individualized ego
is a span passing man's comprehension.   Born from
a purely spiritual condition into mortality, as we
might say, it is now reborn into the spiritual state
on a vastly different plane of progression.   This is
undoubtedly the true exegesis of Jesus' words to
Nicodemus, "Verily I say unto you except a man
be born of Water (the material world, all forms of
life in which came originally from water or original
slime), and of the Spirit (rebirth, greatly developed
and progressed, into spiritual life), he cannot see
the kingdom," etc.   And again, "Ye must be born
again."   Nicodemus could not conceive of entering his mother's womb and being born again;
neither can we conceive how the mere application

of water, spiritually or otherwise, constitutes new birth, but it is not difficult to understand this through the natural process of rebirth into a higher and better phase of life. It is probable that the old legend of the "Fall of Man" had its origin in this very conception, for the ideas herein expressed are not essentially new except in their application.

To the ancients, the incarnation of Spirit in mortal form symbolized the Fall of Spirit from what they considered its high estate; becoming degraded by contact with mortality; and this idea soon found expression in the doctrine of the "Fall of Man," which we find incorporated into all the ancient rituals. This is not surprising when we remember that in the doctrine of reincarnation, as held by all orientals, Spirit is assumed to be the only true state of existence, and mortality is considered of such low estate that it is looked upon rather as a form of punishment to be borne patiently and passed through as quickly as possible, and as many times as may be necessary, until the soul is finally fitted for Nirvana.

It would hardly be possible for us to pass this subject of Reincarnation without giving it more than passing attention. Today, the subject of occultism in general is occupying so much of our time and thought, that this doctrine of Reincarnation has proved a stumbling block to many and a bone of

contention between widely differing schools.   Aside
from the ignorant few who hopelessly confound
it with the doctrine of transmigration, or the passing of the human soul into lower animal forms, a
great many earnest thinkers cannot solve satisfac-
torily the problems it presents.   The reason for
this is undoubtedly that most thinkers and searchers
along occult and esoteric lines, draw for inspiration
only from the oriental writings.   India is not, nor
has it ever been, infallible as a source of information, yet most schools of today look to that coun-
try as the fount of all wisdom.   Sages of the entire East have always taught many things which
our western philosophy has been slow to grasp, but
in all the ages past, the oriental minds have not
been able to carry to their final solution the subtle
intricacies of metaphysics in the logical manner
peculiar to western intellects.

While it is true that Reincarnation, as a doctrine,
has been held and taught for upwards of five thousand years, and is so held today by a majority of
the religious population of the world, there has
been practically no attempt to gain a clearer conception of its meaning, except by a comparative
few.   Briefly summed up, its principal tenet may
be expressed as the necessity of the continuous Reincarnation of the spiritual Ego in human or mortal
form, until sufficient experience has been gained

to permit it to pursue its development on a purely spiritual plane, where, after it has attained the requisite purity, it enters Nirvana, and thence after endless cycles is absorbed into the Supreme. It is no wonder that many western minds find this idea hard to assimilate, for whether we say absorption or annihilation, the terms in this case are practically synonymous. If absorption into the Supreme means the merging of individuality (losing oneself in the Supreme is the term often employed) then all our struggle for endless ages to gain spiritual experience and developmnt by physical progression has been a colossal economic waste of energy—a psychological crime. But considered by the aid of that Light we are seeking, it is possible we shall not find this to be the case. After carefully considering the premises let us admit three basic facts:

First—All life is a state of progression both on spiritual and physical planes.

Second—The purpose of mortal existence is to furnish opportunity for primordial Spirit Matter to become individualized, through a set of experiences or environments, until it becomes a distinct entity or ego; and that in view of the average duration of a given physical environment, it is obviously impossible for any ego to exhaust the possibilities of development in a single expression or incarnation.

Third—That the purpose of the Spirit entity, whether consciously expressed or not, is to utilize to the utmost all the experiences with which it may come into contact or rapport.

Now is it reasonable to assume, that since Spirit is immortal, without beginning and without ending, and for an eternity past it has been progressing toward a given point in time, that on the attainment of individuality it has accomplished all that its high destiny requires? Few would be hardy enough to say that a single mortal life-time, with its varying experiences and conditions, would be sufficient for all eternity, past, present and future. With sociological conditions which, under varying presentations, are practically the same in all ages, constantly before us, can we assume for a moment that every Spirit that passes through mortal experience, has equal opportunities with every other Spirit? Yet, having a desire to avail itself to the utmost of all the development that mortality can give, can we conceive it any part of the eternal Law of Justice that three score years and ten shall constitute the gauge of that experience? Nature has provided for us whatever is needful for our complete development, and if conditions under which a human being comes into existence are not such as to allow that ego the fullest opportunity of development and expansion, then we may be sure

that provision has been made for just such lack
of opportunity. But since life displays its activities along the strict line of evolution and progression, we may be sure that it will be necessary for
us to incorporate our ego into a new human em-
bryo and undergo again the necessity of mortal
birth. Since the state of mortality is necessary
to furnish the experiences required by the Spirit
Entity, it is certain that contact with the mortal
must in some way take place. This being so, what
more logical for us to assume than that, when we
have passed through the transition we call death,
we should look backward from the wider outlook
of the spiritual plane and review the set of experiences through which we had just passed. What
more logical than that we should select those which
are needful for our completer development in the
environment which shall later attach to, or surround our human organism, about to commence its
journey toward rebirth or reincarnation for another
mortal or human expression. By so doing we
should work out according to the law of Karma,
or as we prefer to call it, the law of Ripe Causa-
tion, the errors of previous existences, and accumu-
late and assimilate experience to be digested, absorbed and utilized in future existences. And this
process is to continue not indefinitely, but until
the Ego has been privileged to experience all the

conditions to which mortality is subject. Only
then is it in a condition or position to begin its
final and exclusive progress on the spiritual planes,
its ultimate destiny that of becomng one of the
Creative Hierarchies.

Is it not obvious that thus we could logically
account for the many cases of dual and even mul-
tiple personality which perplex our psychologists?
Would it not account for the Lincolns who, from
obscurity or under adverse conditions, rise to supremacy among their fellow men, urged on by the
unseen yet ever present force, guidance and wisdom, of an ego who perhaps had already fought
life's battles before? Many of the sociological
problems of today would cease to be such, could
we rightly understand and grasp this idea. And
if we understand rightly the presence of the Unseen
Brotherhood who silently work for Humanity by
training' and guiding many of these advanced egos,
incarnate for the time being, we should realize how
many of the great movements inaugurated in each
generation, owe their impetus and activity to the
intelligent direction of those who, having completed
life's course, now function on the spiritual planes
for those still following the pathway of the flesh.

It may be said that this is mere speculation. Possibly so, for we can never surely know until each
has passed the veil which ever shrouds the Un-

seen. Yet it is possible for those whose incarnations are nearly completed, to arrive at such a stage of initiation and development as to become conscious, while still incarnate of their previous existences.

It is not idle for us to inquire about these things, for honest inquiry and philosophic investigations enlarge our spiritual conceptions and make for a broader mentality. We have cause for thankfulness that we have been fortunate enough to witness in this dawn of a new century, such a drawing together of the two worlds, physical and spiritual, as a result of scientific investigation, a determined disregard for the shackles of ecclesiasticism, and a thirst for information upon such all important topics among the great masses of mankind, as has never before been known. The basic truths of psychic phenomena are now accepted by the greatest scientists the world over. Many of those truths have been reduced to scientific laws and are in the category of demonstrable facts. That they have at least made their impress upon the world's thought and literature, and consequently upon its work in general, can no longer be denied.

THE WORD, THE LIGHT, THE SELF.

The day of the supernatural is passing. That only is supernatural which pertains to our present state of being. And the supernatural is, in reality, only the unexplained natural. When we comprehend the totality of Spirit, it is difficult for us to formulate any conception which will adequately explain to us the necessity for mortality. From evolution we learn that its pathway is marked by gradations ranging from the invisible planes down through planes more and more objective, until in the human it would seem that Matter had attained its highest development. But we see, too, that from the visible or mortal state, we pass onwards, higher, but back into the invisible or spiritual realms of being. The true conception of our state of being and the supernatural, is most succinctly stated by Richard Jefferies: "Realizing that Spirit, recognizing my own Inner Consciousness, the psyche so clearly, I cannot understand time. It is eternity now. I am in the midst of it. It is about me in the sunshine; I am in it as the butterfly floats in the light-laden air. Nothing has to come; it is now. Now is eternity; now is the immortal life. Here this moment, by this tumulus, on earth, now, I exist in it. The years, the centuries, the cycles, are absolutely nothing; it is only a moment since this tumulus was raised; in a thousand years more it will still be only a moment. To the soul there is no Past and no Future; all is, and will be ever in, Now. For artificial purposes time is mutually agreed on, but there is really no such thing. The shadow goes on upon the dial, the index moves round upon the clock, and what is the difference? None whatever. If the clock had never been set going, what would have been the difference? There may be time for the clock, the clock may make time for itself; there is none for me.

"I dip my hand in the brook and feel the stream; in an instant the particles of water which first touched me have floated yards down the current; my hand remains there. I take my hand away, and the flow—the time of the brook—does not exist to me. The great clock of the firmament, the sun and the stars, the crescent moon, the earth circling two thousand times, are no more to me than the flow of the brook when my hand is withdrawn; my soul has never been, and never can be, dipped in time. Time has never existed, and never will; it is a purely artificial arrangement. It is eternity now; it always was eternity, and always will be.

By no possible means could I get into time if I tried. I am in eternity now, and must there remain. Haste not, be at rest; this NOW is eternity. Because the idea of time has left my mind—if ever it had any hold on it—to me the man interred in the tumulus is living now, as I live. We are both in eternity.

"There is no separation, no Past; eternity, the NOW, is continuous. When all the stars have revolved they only produce NOW again. The continuity of NOW is forever. So that it appears to me purely natural, and not supernatural, that the soul whose temporary frame was interred in this mound should be existing as I sit on the sward. How infinitely deeper is thought than the million miles of the firmament! The wonder is here, not there; now—not to be—now always. Things that have been miscalled supernatural appear to me simple, more natural than Nature, than earth, than sea, or sun. It is beyond telling, more natural that I should have a soul than not, that there should be immortality. I think there is much more than immortality. It is matter which is the supernatural, and difficult of understanding. Why this clod of earth I hold in my hand? Why this water which drops sparkling from my fingers dipped in the brook? Why are they at all? When? How? What for? Matter is beyond understanding, mys-

terious, impenetrable. I touch it easily; comprehend it—no. Soul, mind—the thought—the idea
—is easily understood; it understands itself and is
conscious.

"The supernatural miscalled—the natural in truth
is the real. To me everything is supernatural.
How strange that condition of mind which cannot
accept anything but the earth, the sea, the tangible
universe! Without the misnamed supernatural
these seem to me incomplete, unfinished. Without
soul all these are dead."[10]

Does not this simple appeal of a human soul
struggling in the light of the Inner Illumination rend
all mystery from the so-called supernatural? Does
it not reveal to us the existence of a consciousness
of conditions more genuinely real, tangible, and
lasting than what we are pleased to call the normal
consciousness would seem to indicate to us? WHO
is it, in our mortal framework that senses this condition? WHO ARE WE, each individually? By
WHAT POWER does this Inner Being sense these
pregnant truths? And finally, WHAT IS THE
TRUTH it senses?

Twenty thousand years ago, the Caveman paused
in his works of Operative Masonry, and in the
faint dawn of human reason, scarcely able to com-

---

[10] The Story of My Heart.   —Richard Jefferies.

prehend the Light that was slowly but surely dawning upon him, wrested from the unknown, yet
feebly appreciated sources of the inspiration of
the great Book of Creation whose pages lay spread
before him, three distinct truths.   These three
truths were, the comprehension of the Creative Fiat;
the existence of himself as the product of that
Word; and the Light to perceive his relationship
(mystically to him though it might be), to his
Creator.   And in all the ages from that remote
time to our own period, his successors have been
struggling to cherish that Light, and by its aid to
gain a larger vision of the eternal verities of being.   Is not the mystery, if such it be, revealed to
us in these lines?   Can we not see that the Great
Ultimate Trinity, the Word, the Light, and the
Self, stand out no longer as an impersonal trio, but
as the Three in One, of which Man himself is the
incarnate expression?   Can we not see that neither
in the mystic OM-AUM of Brahminism, nor in any
modern combination of sounds or symbols is to be
found the true understanding of the Master's Word?
Knowing as we do, with the results of science's
crowning achievements at our hand, as proof that
electricity and magnetism, heat, light, sound, cold,
Matter and Spirit are one and the same FORCE
in varying modes of motion, all in their ultimate
analysis, but differing manifestations of that Force,

and that Force but the Activity of the Supreme and
Eternal WILL, back of and ordering all—is it not
obvious that the Omnific Word itself, is but the
primal vibration of the Eternal Will?   Through all
the ages this Word has found conscious expression
in reasoning man, revealing itself to us in the lower
stages of its development as the physical phenomena of being, evidenced to us through the avenues of sense perception; and in the higher stages
of its evolution demonstrating our AT-ONE-MENT
with Eternal Will.   Hence we are truly sons of
God, each in his own nature, divine.   Can we not
see further, that the same vibration is also the Mystic
Light, revealing to us objective conditions through
our physical senses, and to our finer and more subtle sensorium, the truth of our Divine Selfhood?
Thus each human unit is seen to be an integral portion of the Eternal One.   Thus is torn from our
eyes the cobwebs of dogmatic formularies of dam-
nation, salvation, redemption, and all other fetters
which have been formulated to hold men's intellects in ecclesiastical thralldom.   We cannot conceive of a material heaven, any more than we can
conceive of the opposites of good and evil as
tangible conditions, realizing as we do that they
are purely relative conditions in any given code
of ethics at any time.

The world is ready for a new gospel.   From the

material religious systems of the past, appealing to the sensual and aesthetic emotions, to the speculative philosophies of today, the world has cried out for something satisfying to its mental capacities and affording a reasonable working basis for its every day ethics.

In all the ages past, from the high priests of old, to the theologians of today, honest inquiry and investigation along lines of spiritual thought has been crucified on the cross of ostracism and public opinion. Through it all, however, the Divine Light of this last and greatest trinity has shed its beams in bright flashes, piercing the intellectual obscurity of the centuries, encouraging the daring thinkers of all times to persist in their demands for Truth, and revealing to us in these latter days, the Self, in its Divine relationship to its Creator; that real Self, that is the individual Spirit, which, evolving through all the ages, contains within itself the sum of all experiences and the potentialities of untold development in the future.

Do we not gain some conception of the plans which were laid down upon the Trestle Board of the Supreme Grand Lodge on high? Can we not read from them the purpose of man's creation— to serve a Mission of Divine Mediumship, whereby through him, God, the Eternal Will, the Sovereign Magus of the Universe becomes individualized

Spirit; and again, through man, individualized Spirit returns to its Creative Source.

To the true Seer there is no death, for though he knows that the temporary association with Spirit in its lower forms of visible Matter must be relinquished, he also knows that such transition shall be conscious and that he lies down in slumber, only to be raised by the contact with the higher spiritual forces into the conscious activities of a vastly higher and superlative state of being. Thus he becomes able, while still in the flesh, to rise superior to conditions pertaining to the flesh, and to see, like the Mesu of old, ahead into those realms which, to the uninitiated, must remain at least during their mortal expressions, invisible.

May those WHO HAVE SEEN, each, by constant thought and desire, strive to hasten the approach of that true millenium, wherein mankind shall have emerged from the obscuring clouds of commercialism, materialism, and ecclesiasticism, and by a rational development of the spiritual faculties, realize that Man, though in the midst of mortality, is in immortality.

Let no true student of the occult believe for a moment that in the I H V H, the Yod, He, Vau, He or Hebrew Ineffable Name, he has discovered that which must always be undiscoverable—the Master's Word. The true Initiate seeks not to "discover" that which was NEVER lost. Treatment of this subject through the printed page necessarily enjoins extreme caution. Let us point out, however, that the "First Vibration" of Infinite Mind still exists. We are the results and containers of the "First Vibration." He who "discovers" himself will be conscious of possessing the true Word.

"In the beginning was the Logos, and the Logos was with God, and the Logos WAS God." "The Logos was made flesh, and dwelt among men." Centuries ago the fiat went forth, "O Man, Know thyself." He who "knows" himself will recognize the incarnation of the Logos, and wherein it dwells among men.

"In every city there be two or three Mekubbalim." Some will understand that the Word which was never spoken, can still be heard by those who are willing to "put themselves in a proper position" to hear it.

May the Word be heard; the Light shine forth; the Self be revealed through these pages, in such wise that some thereby shall be advanced along the pathway of true spiritual development and revelation, and be brought into closer communion with the two worlds, Seen and Unseen.